KNOWLEDGE REPRESENTATION AND LANGUAGE IN AI

KNOWLEDGE REPRESENTATION AND LANGUAGE IN AI

J. P. E. HODGSON   BA, MA, PhD
Center for Machine Learning
Department of Mathematics and Computer Science
Saint Joseph's University, Philadelphia, USA

ELLIS HORWOOD
NEW YORK   LONDON   TORONTO   SYDNEY   TOKYO   SINGAPORE

First published in 1991 by
ELLIS HORWOOD LIMITED
Market Cross House, Cooper Street,
Chichester, West Sussex, PO19 1EB, England

A division of
Simon & Schuster International Group
A Paramount Communications Company

Printed and bound in Great Britain
by Bookcraft Limited, Midsomer Norton, Avon

British Library Cataloguing in Publication Data

Hodgson, J.P.E.
Knowledge representation and language in AI.
CIP catalogue record for this book is available from the British Library
ISBN 0–13–515123–6   1/93

Library of Congress Cataloging-in-Publication Data available

Contents

Chapter 1

Introduction

The focus of this book is on the relationship between knowledge representation and language in Artificial Intelligence. More particularly upon the way in which the choice of representation influences the language used to discuss a problem and vice-versa.

For some time now the trend in Artificial Intelligence has been towards systems in which knowledge is separate from procedure. The analogy with relational database theory is often used. In database applications access to the data is constrained to be entirely through the database manager. Programs that use the data do not have access to the internal structure of the database itself. This permits modification of the data to be separated from the maintenance of the program that processes the data. The analogous structure in Artificial Intelligence would provide a Knowledge Base manager through which an inference engine would access the system's knowledge without access to the internal structure of the knowledge.

This kind of modularization is of course much older than the database application. Program design has long called for separation of data from code. But there is more to this separation than merely keeping the two in separate places. The division must be a structured in a meaningful way. As an example of this consider the use of abstract data types to encapsulate the structure of data. This methodology has been used in program design for quite some time now. At one level it can be viewed as a logical extension of the layered approach to system design. Just as an operating system kernel provides an extension to the "native language" of the hardware so an abstract data type may be regarded as providing a new elementary data type in a language together with the language for talking about it.

This sense that one works in the context of some extended language provides a very powerful way of addressing programming problems. The process of writing a program becomes one of "choosing the right words" for the purpose at hand. However there are limits to the process of continually extending a language. Much criticism of the Ada[1] is based on a feeling that the language is too large. Many successful languages are quite small. This is quite apparent in AI. The dominant languages of AI, which I shall take to be LISP, Prolog, Smalltalk and C – a position that I hope to justify in this book – are all small in the sense that they rely on few language elements. This makes them "graspable". I believe that this sense that one can encompass the language needed to describe a problem adequately is perhaps the most important part of being able to solve it.

It is essential to have a conceptually simple language for AI applications because these applications are usually systems that must cope with large quantities of (usually ill structured) data. Expert systems acquire new rules to handle new situations. Natural language is bedeviled by numerous exceptions. Vision has to cope with massive amounts of data. In each of these cases one of the central problems is that of coordinating the knowledge that the system has. Moreover this coordination must permit efficient access. An AI application must therefore provide languages for accessing and organising the knowledge upon which it is based. The point of this book is that the language is inevitably linked to the knowledge representation method.

Although simplicity of language may be desirable this does not preclude the construction of higher level interfaces to an AI system. Just as one can address a relational database through a sequence of screen queries and in so doing achieve good results so one can build sophisticated interfaces to AI systems. It is the presence of a clear conceptual model in the background that will make this possible.

I should emphasise that a total separation of knowledge and procedure is not always desirable. There will be cases in which an under-

---

[1]Ada is a trademark of the Department of Defense

standing of the internal structure of the knowledge base is necessary. Such would be the case when the capacity of the system is severely taxed and some form of reorganisation is required. However even in those cases where information about the internal structure is necessary the language that is used to manipulate the knowledge should provide the hooks necessary to reveal the structure. The intimate relationship between representation and the language most properly used to describe it provides just the right kind of "leakage" of information from the knowledge base to the rest of the system.

1.1 Structure of the Book

I want to use this book to explore this relationship between language, representation and reason in some detail. Indeed I can state the main thesis as follows

> The right language provides all the information needed concerning the representation and organisation of a knowledge base.

If this thesis is correct – and I believe it is – then the structure of the book should develop logically from this thesis.

I begin with a discussion of knowledge representation methods. I do not give an exhaustive survey of all the methods, preferring to concentrate on a small subset. The reader should be warned that this subset will not include neural networks. I omit these not because they do not support my position, but rather because I have a number of reservations about the degree to which they may be said to represent knowledge. Most applications with which I am familiar seem to depend on some prior decision as to what is significant. It seems to me that semantic nets can be made to carry this part of the representational content of neural nets.

I follow this with a discussion of reasoning methods. It is here that I can begin to make the case for the intimate relationship between language and representation. I shall show how each representation method fits particularly well with some reasoning methods and less so with others. In making this case for the relationship between languages and reasoning I will use specific languages as examples. It is here that I will justify my earlier claim about the languages that seem good for AI.

Even though I have been insisting on a strong relationship between language, reasoning and representation, it is the case that there different ways of representing problems. The question of representation change is an important one, especially as my thesis would seem to require that there must also be a language change to go along with it. In fact this is a complex issue about which not nearly enough is known. By gathering together some recent work in problem solving I will show how, in some cases it has been possible to use representation changes to recast problems into a language that makes them easier to solve.

In these first chapters all the discussion has been at what one might characterise as the level of "micro AI"[2]. One of the standard questions that is asked in AI is "Does it scale up?". Any serious work in AI must eventually address this problem. I maintain that the relationships that this book explores lie at the heart of the construction of large systems. To prove this I will examine a number of the current large AI systems from the viewpoint of representation and language.

In particular I will examine three large systems: ALICE [63] which was constructed by Jean Louis Lauriére and was amongst the first implementations of a problem solving system able to attack many problems; **Soar** [61] developed at Carnegie-Mellon University by John Laird, Paul Rosenbloom and Alan Newell; lastly the Cyc system [66] which is being developed by Douglas Lenat and his collaborators. Each of these systems is sufficiently well developed that it is possible to discuss them from my viewpoint. This consideration of large systems also contains a brief discussion of blackboard systems and the use of hypertext like interfaces.

I conclude the book with a review of the argument for the centrality of both language and representation in AI. As we shall see it is the role of language to manipulate concepts and of representation to support access to both general and specific cases of the concepts within the knowledge base. The discussion focusses on the questions of representation, inference, control, and the closed world assumption.

---

[2]In the same sense as Microeconomics

Throughout the book I introduce notions from the mathematical theory called category theory. I do this because it is my belief that this viewpoint has much to offer AI. Category theory is in a real sense about "pure structure" which fits it for trying to determine the problem independent part of problem solving. There is much that remains to be done in the area, but it is already clear that the approach has value. [81], [11], and [20] amongst others provide evidence of this.

References

The bibliographic references appear at the end of the book. The appear by alphabetical order of the authors of the cited work. In addition they are numbered to permit the reader to locate them from the body of the text.

Acknowledgements

I could never have written this book without the unflagging encouragement of Ranan Banerji. His willingness to listen to me at any and all times provided much needed support. Paul Benjamin and Mike Lowry sustained my belief in the categorical approach.

Chapter 2

Knowledge Representation

In this chapter I will review the some of the fundamental methods of knowledge representation. These are logic, productions systems, semantic networks and frame hierarchies. The approach that I take is very much one of overview. The reader who is interested in more details should consult the references provided in the text.

I have tried to focus on a small number of common problems that will arise with any system of knowledge representation. Chief amongst these is the problems of conflicting information. The examples that I have chosen as should serve as illustrations of this concern.

2.1 Logic

John McCarthy [70] was one of the first persons to advocate the use of logic for knowledge representation. He was specifically concerned to build systems that would be able to reason about the world. In his language a programme "has common sense if it automatically deduces for itself a sufficiently wide class of immediate consequences of anything it is told and what it already knows."

Our goal here limited to showing how logic is used for the specific purpose of knowledge representation. A more comprehensive introduction to the use of logic in Artificial Intelligence can be found in [97].

Logic serves to carry declarative knowledge rather than procedural knowledge. What is, rather than a prescription for bringing a situation about.

2.1.1   Classical Logics

Ultimately the logical representation of knowledge is based upon the classical predicate calculus. For example, we can express our knowledge about a person X's religious beliefs and political convictions as follows.

Religion(X,Quaker) and PartyAffiliation(X,Republican)

Statements of this kind make up the predicate calculus. The foundation of the predicate calculus is the concept of a *well-formed formula* or *wff* for short. The syntax rules of the predicate calculus specify the ways of combining the language elements into wffs. The reasoning power of predicate calculus is based upon a collection of axioms and inference rules which describe the ways in which new wffs can be deduced from a given set of wffs.

The language of the predicate calculus is given by a set of variables $x_0, \ldots x_i, \ldots$ together with, for each $n > 0$, a set R_n of n-place relation symbols and a set f_n of n-place function symbols. The number n is called the arity of the relation or function. In addition to these symbols there are the logical connectives $\vee$, $\wedge$, $\sim$, $\rightarrow$, $\leftrightarrow$, the quantifiers $\forall$ and $\exists$. Wffs are constructed from atomic wffs using the logical connectives and quantifiers. Atomic wffs built from *terms*. A term is

- a variable,

- $f(s_1, \ldots, s_m)$ where the s_i are terms and f is a function symbol.

An atomic wff is any expression of the form $C(t_1, \ldots, t_n)$ where C is relation of arity n, and each t_i is a term.

The rules for combining atomic wffs into more complex wffs are as follows.

If A and B are wffs so are

1. $\sim A$

2. $A \vee B$

3. $A \wedge B$

4. $A \rightarrow B$

5. $A \leftrightarrow B$

6. $\forall x \ A$

7. $\exists x \ A$

The axioms of the predicate calculus can then be stated as follows.
Axioms for the Predicate Calculus
For any wffs A, B, C

1. $A \rightarrow (B \rightarrow A)$

2. $(A \rightarrow (B \rightarrow C)) \rightarrow ((A \rightarrow B) \rightarrow (A \rightarrow C))$

3. $(\sim B \rightarrow \sim A) \rightarrow ((\sim B \rightarrow A) \rightarrow B)$

4. $\forall x A(x) \rightarrow A(t)$ where t is a term such that no unbound occurrences of x in A lie in the scope of any quantifier in t

5. $(\forall x)(A \rightarrow B) \rightarrow (A \rightarrow \forall x B)$ where A contains no free occurrence of x.

If we follow the usual convention in which inference rules are written in the form

$$\frac{Hypotheses}{Conclusion}$$

meaning that the hypotheses given above the line imply the conclusion below the line then the inference rules for predicate calculus take the form:
Inference Rules for Predicate Calculus
Modus Ponens

$$\frac{A \quad A \rightarrow B}{B}$$

Generalisation

$$\frac{A}{\forall x A}$$

A *proof* is any sequence of the form $A_1, \ldots, A_n$ where each A_i is either an instance of an axiom or follows from earlier members of the sequence using either modus ponens or generalisation. A *theorem* is any wff which is the last member of a proof sequence.

I will defer further discussion of proof methods until chapter 3, for the moment I am concerned with the representational aspects of the predicate calculus. We began with a representation of categorical information using predicate calculus. We now take this further (to a point where some difficulties become apparent) as follows.

Suppose that we want to represent the configuration of objects in a room. This will be necessary for the case where we wish to construct an intelligent agent that is able to move about the room without banging into things. Indeed this was one of McCarthy's original intentions in introducing logic as a form of knowledge representation. The agent would be able to use the inference rules of logic to reason about its environment.

I have assumed the existence of some primitive concepts – at, on, and between – in terms of which it is possible to define the more complex notion "CanGoFromTo" using only the rules of the predicate calculus.

at(door, robot)
at(window, table)
between(door, window, chair)
on(table, item)
$\sim$ ($\exists$Obstacle between(Start, Finish, Obstacle)) $\rightarrow$
CanGoFromTo(Agent, Start, Finish)

At first it seems natural to hope that this kind of approach can provide ways to describe complex situations. The next example shows that things will not work out quite as smoothly as we hope. We suppose the following information.

Religion(X, QUaker) $\rightarrow$ Pacifist(X)
PartyAffiliation(X, Republican) $\rightarrow$ Advocates(X, strong defense)
Advocates(X, strong defense) $\rightarrow$ $\sim$Pacifist(X)

If on the basis of this knowledge we are asked "Is there a Quaker whose party affiliation is republican", that is to try and deduce the truth of

$$\exists X \text{ Religion}(X, \text{Quaker}) \wedge \text{PartyAffiliation}(X, \text{Republican})$$

we find that we arrive at a contradiction in that we get both Pacifist(X) and ~Pacifist(X). Since this kind of ambiguous conclusion is frequent in real life any intelligent agent must have a way to cope with it. In the next section we describe some of the approaches that have been suggested for handling this kind of difficulty.

2.1.2 Modal Logics

Many of the difficulties in using classical logic for knowledge representation arise because of the absolute nature of the deduction rules. This does not allow for the more tentative nature of human reasoning and its ability to tolerate a level of contradiction. Thus most humans are quite happy with the statements about Quakers and Republicans given earlier. When they meet a Quaker commander in chief they are able to modify their belief system to account for this. In doing so, and this is critically important for normal reasoning, they do not abandon the initial assumptions about Quakers and Republicans in general. How can one do this in the context of a logic for AI? Modal logics provide one way of doing this. Part of their attraction is that they provide an intuitively plausible basis for constructing the semantics. This is done at the expense of introducing new rules of inference. Many advocates of first order logic maintain that it is not really necessary to do this [28] since one can introduce suitable predicates into the first order system to describe the situation. The practical truth seems to lie somewhere in between. The modal logics provide a language for dealing with specific concepts. That the same can be achieved in first order logic should be regarded as a bonus since it permits the translation of known results from first order logic into a given modal system. I have in mind specifically questions of completeness and soundness of reasoning methods.

Typically modal logic introduces *modal operators* L and M that are applied to wffs. If A is a wff then the wff LA can be interpreted as meaning 'it is necessary that A' and the wff MA can be interpreted as meaning 'possibly A'. L and M thus provide a way of distinguishing 'necessary' truths from 'contingent' truths. Thus advocates of a strong defense are necessarily not pacificists, but Quakers are not necessarily pacificists, or in predicate terms we have

$$L((\text{advocates}(X, \text{strong defense}) \rightarrow \sim\text{pacifist}(X))$$
$$M(\exists X \text{ religion}(X, \text{Quaker}) \wedge \sim \text{pacifist}(X))$$

There are a number of possible additional inference rules for the modifiers L and M each of which give rise to different modal logics. The precise choice is dependent upon the application. The reader is referred to [97] and the references therein for more details.

A more formal understanding of the interpretation of a modal logic is given by the use of possible world models. These models provide a semantics for modal logic. The modal logic provides a representation of these worlds.

Definition 2.1.1 *A modal frame is a structure* $(W, \ D, \ R, \ F)$ *where*

1. *W is a non-empty set (the possible worlds);*

2. *D is a non-empty domain of individuals;*

3. *R is a binary relation of 'accessibility' on W;*

4. *F is a function which assigns to each pair consisting of a function symbol f of arity $n \geq 0$ and an element $w \epsilon W$, a function $F(f) : D^n \rightarrow D$, and to each pair (C, w) consisting of a relation C of arity $n \geq 0$ and an element $w \epsilon W$ an element $F(C, w)$ of 2^{D^n}.*

The function F thus assigns the value of each f and relation R depending upon the possible world w. The accessibility relation has the following interpretation. If w_1 and w_2 are elements of W such that $w_1 R w_2$ then the accessibility of w_1 from w_2 should be seen as meaning that in the context of w_2 the observations of w_1 are consistent, whereas if a world is not accessible from w_2 its observations will be in some way inconsistent with those of w_2.

We can illustrate how this might be used in the context of or earlier discussion of between. We can make the following assertions about the predicate 'between', where $between(X, Y, Z)$ is interpreted as meaning Z is between X and Y.

$$L(\text{between}(A,D,B), \text{between}(B,D,C) \rightarrow \text{between}(A,D,C)$$
$$M(\text{between}(A,D,B), \text{between}(B,D,C) \rightarrow \text{between}(C,A,D)$$

To see that the second is possible imagine that the points A, B, C and D are arranged around a circle. The first line then represents a necessary property of 'betweenness' as it is conventionally understood. Thus one which must be true in all worlds. Whereas the second line represents a property that can be true in some worlds but not all.

If we were to make the world explicit by introducing a predicate that indicated that the points indeed lay on a circle we could achieve the same result without the introduction of the modal operators. But just as one is not obliged to program in machine code when higher level languages are available so one is not obligated to use first order logic all the time.

2.1.3   Fuzzy Logics

In the construction of real world AI systems it is imperative to take account of the vagueness inherent in normal discourse. Most of the concepts that we use for everyday communication are not "crisp" in the sense that they admit of a precise specification. Thus we say.

> John is tall.

When we say this we will usually be understood, even though we have not specified an exact height for John. The problem becomes even more serious when we consider statements such as:

> John is rather tall.

On the other hand it allows us to make the statements.

> Most Quakers are pacifists.
> Most Republicans advocate a strong defense.

While these two statements do not immediately resolve the Quaker-Republican problem they do leave open the possibility of a non-pacifist Quaker, or a Pacifist Republican. How then should one formalise this?

The formalization of informal reasoning is called 'fuzzification' and proceeds in two stages. The ideas are originally due to Zadeh

([103] and [104]). I shall proceed by drawing an analogy with classical logic. In Negoita's book [73] he carries out this analogy on a formal categorical level, what follows is a version of this without the category theory.

One conventional interpretation of classical logic is in terms of the algebra of subsets of some universe. Indeed the possible worlds of modal logic are examples of this approach. The foundation of set theory is the membership relation[1]. The process of fuzzification begins with the membership relation itself. Rather than the 'crisp' binary yes or no of classical logic one has degrees of membership.

More formally if U is the universe of discourse and P is a classical predicate then P determines a subset $S_P = \{u \epsilon U \mid P(u) = 1\}$, and each subset S of U determines a predicate P_S given by $P_S(u) = 1$ iff $u \epsilon S$. In fuzzy logic a predicate is a function from U to the interval $[0, 1]$. In order to preserve the analogy with classical logic a fuzzy set A is defined to be a function $U_A : U \rightarrow [0, 1]$.

With this definition one can define the notion of subset, intersection and union as follows.

Let A, B be fuzzy subsets of U then define

Subsets

$$A \subset B \Leftrightarrow (\forall u \epsilon U)(U_A(u) \leq U_B(u))$$

Intersection

$$U_{A \cap B}(u) = Min(U_A(u), U_B(u))$$

Union

$$U_{A \cap B}(u) = Max(U_A(u), U_B(u))$$

Complementation

A and B are complementary if
$$U_B(u) = 1 - U_A(u)$$

At this point it may appear that fuzzification has made things more precise rather than less so. However by choosing an appropriate set of values for the membership functions U_A one can obtain the 'vague' predicates such as 'very', 'most', 'few' and so on. A more effective way to do it is through the introduction of fuzzy logic.

---

[1]Russell's paradox is in one sense an unresolvable membership question.

The fuzzification of logic proceeds in a manner that is exactly analogous to the fuzzification of sets, that is the 'truth function' itself is fuzzified. The truth value set has a countable set of values

{true, false, very true, not true, not very true, rather true ...}

These are determined as fuzzy subsets of $[0, 1]$. If we assume that U_{true} is the membership function for the fuzzy subset true, then we might have

$$U_{false}(t) = U_{true}(1 - t)$$

$$U_{nottrue}(t) = 1 - U_{true}(t)$$

$$U_{verytrue}(t) = (U_{true}(t))^2$$

$$U_{rathertrue}(t) = (U_{true}(t))^{1/2}$$

With these preliminaries it is then possible to interpret the logical constants such as $\wedge$, $\vee$, $\sim$, *and* $\rightarrow$. If one works with the function interpretation of fuzziness it is quite straightforward to provide interpretations of each of these concepts. However this is not what one wants to do. Rather one wants to be able to draw conclusions such as

> Most Quakers are pacifists
> Richard is a Quaker
> ————————————————
> It is likely that Richard is a pacifist.

Zadeh uses what he calls *Linguistic Approximation* whereby each fuzzy subset S of $[0, 1]$ has associated with it an element of the set of truth values. It is not clear how this best approximation is to be chosen, and in general the set of truth values is itself somewhat determined by the application context. For example in the case of or robot and its location there would be use for a predicate 'near'. Further the robot would need a different version of near from that required by an autonomous vehicle.

In concluding our discussion of fuzzy logic we remark that the notion of fuzzy set is quite precise given the presence of a precise part of fuzzy logic. The vagueness is embedded in the linguistic approximation. Perhaps there should be a name for the underlying precise theory that does not carry the connotations that "fuzzy" does.

It is also worth noting that the final translation to the everyday vague predicates is explicitly called a linguistic approximation. Fuzzy logic is thus quite clear about its desire to provide a language for talking about vague predicates. In this sense it shares some of the features of a modal logic. We see once again the desire to provide a first order language for describing concepts that in classical logic require considerable additional structure. For fuzzy concepts such as "very" the goal seems more elusive than that of providing a meaning for "possibly" and "necessarily".

2.1.4   Intuitionistic Logics

Intuitionistic logic rightly plays a significant role in computer science in general and in AI in particular because of its emphasis upon constructibility. The essence of intuitionism is that a proposition is only true if a constructive proof of it exists. Given this we can interpret the classical logical connectives according to the following table, (taken from [97].)

Proposition	Proof
$A \vee B$	A proof of A or of B
$A \wedge B$	A proof of A and a proof of B
$A \rightarrow B$	A construction which transforms any given proof of A into one for B.
$\sim A$	A proof of $A \rightarrow \perp$ where $\perp$ is some absurd statement such as $(0 = 1)$
$\exists x\ A(x)$	A construction of $A(c)$ for some individual c
$\forall x\ A(x)$	A construction which when applied to any individual c yields a proof of $A(c)$

The particular relevance of this to my thesis will become clearer in the chapter on language. For the moment I can illustrate its effectiveness in the area of knowledge representation with some examples.

In intuitionistic logic before we can assert

$$\text{religion(X, Quaker)} \rightarrow \text{pacifist(X)}$$

we need a constructive proof of the implication. Similarly for the assertion

$$\text{PartyAffiliation(X, Republican)} \rightarrow \text{advocates(X, strong defense)}$$
$$\text{advocates(X, strong defense)} \rightarrow \sim \text{pacifist(X)}$$

The existence of a non pacifist Republican Quaker would presumably block the proof of the first of these implications. Intuitionistic reasoning thus very explicitly forbids default reasoning.

2.1.5 Other Logics

I will briefly review a number of other logics that have been used.

Temporal Logic

Temporal logics must deal with the possibility that the truth value of a statement may change with time. This is critically important for the problem of intelligent agents that must interact with an evolving world. In a sense that is comparable to the case of fuzzification there would be no problem if it were possible to determine the time evolution of all the relevant processes and actors. Time independent predicates like *at(door, robot)* could be replaced by ones that are specifically time dependent such as *at(door, robot, t_0)* or even *at(t_0)(robot, door)*. This would, presumably allow one to reason explicitly with the instantaneous predicate values.

This is of course asking too much and so one seeks to find a finitistic solution. Rather in the way that fuzzification is an attempt at a finite solution to the degree of membership problem. I will describe two such attempts.

In the first we draw on the example of modal logic and introduce temporal operators F, P, G, and H. The intuitive interpretation of these operators is as follows

1. $F A$ A is true at some future time.

2. $P A$ A was true at some past time.

3. *GA A* will be true at all future times.

4. *HA A* was true at all past time.

We can use the notion of *temporal frame* to make time explicit. In brief a temporal frame T is a non-empty set of time points, a relation R, of temporal precedence together with a function $h : T \times$ *Atomic Sentences* $\rightarrow \{0,1\}$. We will not spell out the requirements on h the interested reader is referred to [97] for details.

A second method is to introduce the concepts of an event. The idea is that an event has a duration which is an interval in time. At any instant some subset of the events are in progress. Intuitively one wants to describe a process in terms of its component events. Formally this is done through the notion of an event structure [53].

Definition 2.1.2 *An* event structure $E =< E, \sqsubset, O >$ *consists of a non-empty set* E *of events together with the two binary relations,* $\sqsubset$ *representing temporal precedence, and* O *representing overlap, which statisfy the following.*

1. $e_1 \sqsubset e_2 \rightarrow \sim (e_2 O e_1)$;

2. $e_1 \sqsubset e_2 \land e_2 \sqsubset e_3 \rightarrow e_1 \sqsubset e_3$;

3. $(e_1 O e_2) \rightarrow (e_2 O e_1)$;

4. $e_1 O e_1$;

5. $e_1 \sqsubset e_2 \rightarrow \sim (e_1 O e_2)$;

6. $e_1 \sqsubset e_2 \land e_2 \sqsubset e_3 \land e_3 \sqsubset e_4 \rightarrow e_1 \sqsubset e_4$;

7. $e_1 \sqsubset e_2 \lor e_1 O e_2 \lor e_2 \sqsubset e_1$;

With this definition it is possible to give a formal definition of an instant as follows.

Definition 2.1.3 *Let* E *be an event structure. An* instant i *is a subset of* E *such that*

1. $(\forall e_1, e_2 \epsilon \ i)(e_1 O e_2)$

2. $(\forall e_1 \epsilon E \setminus i)(\exists e_2 \epsilon \ i)(\sim (e_1 O e_2))$

The instants are thus the periods of time during which the set of active events is constant. One can try to reason on the event structure using the fact that the instants are temporally ordered.

Three valued logics

A number of three valued logics have been proposed as extensions of classical logic. In principle they all work by providing an additional possible truth-value and a set of truth-tables that describe the semantics of this truth value. The following table describes the intuitive interpretation of the additional value in three example cases [13], [54] , [68]

Logic	Symbol	Interpretation
Bochvar	m	Meaningless
Kleene	u	Undefined
Lukasiewicz	i	Indeterminate

The reader can construct the truth tables for himself based upon these interpretations.

Non-Monotonic Logics

A large problem in Artificial Intelligence applications is that of non-monotonicity. Suppose that we are told that:

Richard is a Quaker.

We will then most likely deduce that Richard is a pacifist. However we may at some later stage in the reasoning turn up new evidence that leads us to the conclusion that he is not in fact a pacifist. How does one deal with this problem? It raises a number of serious issues, one of which is that all conclusions based upon the now falsified assumption are called into question.

A number of methods have been advanced for dealing with this. The most relevant for our purposes is based upon work of Etherington and Reiter [37]. We will describe the ideas in more detail later when we come to the topics of frames and semantic networks, and again in the later discussion of the Cyc system. The main idea is that the knowledge is organised hierarchically so that the chain of reasoning that leads to a particular conclusion can be recovered easily. In this way the evidence supporting a conclusion is in some measure retained with the conclusion. Thus if a link is severed the need to reargue a given conclusion is explicitly evident.

2.1.6 Knowledge Representation in Logic

We can summarize the use of logic for knowledge representation with the following model.

There is a language L, of well-formed expressions. These are the sentences of the language. It is these sentences that are used to make statements about the world. Thus it is this language that 'represents' the knowledge about the world. The specific representation is given by a (semantic) frame, which is a collection of truth values for the predicates of the language applied to a specific set of variables. The frame must respect the axioms of the logic. Conclusions are then to be drawn on the basis of the rules of inference of the logic that is selected as best modeling the situation.

In this context Richard Weyhrauch [99] uses the term simulation structure, a felicitous phrase, which conveys the intention of simulating a portion of the world in the context of a particular logic. In more detail the idea works as follows.

- L is a first order language, based upon predicate symbols P, function symbols F, and constant symbols C. This may include modal or other operators as described above.

- M is a model with domain D.

- S, the *simulation structure* comprises a domain D, predicates P functions F and a distinguished subset C of its domain. It is however strongly restricted since it is intended to serve as a mechanizable analogue of the model. So each predicate is represented by a total algorithm.

From this point of view the task of AI is to build simulation structures in which the algorithms that represent the predicates are tractable, even efficient. I have extended the notion of simulation structure somewhat to permit non standard logics. The language should be first order, since few computer languages permit the graceful use of second order concepts.

The purpose of using logic (in whatever form) as a means of knowledge representation is to provide a language that is versatile enough to cover the concepts that are needed while providing a symbolism that can be manipulated for deductive purposes. In the next chapter we will see how the reasoning attached to a given logic is translated into purely formal terms. But before doing this we have to consider other forms of knowledge representation.

2.2 Production Systems

We can view production systems as a special form of logic based representation. Although this is not perhaps precisely accurate since conventionally a production system involves the inference mechanism as well.

Production systems were first introduced by Emil Post and have found favor as the preferred method of knowledge representation in Expert System Technology. Their first major use in this area came in the the well known diagnostic medical system, MYCIN [29].

Production systems are built from collection of production rules. Each production rule consists of a *condition-action* pair. The interpretation being:

IF *condition* THEN *action*.

It is worth a few words to explain the significance of the term 'production' as it is used in this context. The idea was to be able to give rules that would 'produce' the sentences in a language. So that a production rule would be written

$$LHS \rightarrow RHS$$

meaning that whenever the pattern given by the left hand side was recognised it could be replaced by the one on the right hand side. As an example we can consider the following set of grammar rules.

$$S \rightarrow NP \, VP$$

$$NP \rightarrow Noun$$

$$NP \rightarrow Identifier \, Noun$$

$$VP \rightarrow Verb \, NP$$

$$Identifier \rightarrow \text{``}a\text{''}$$

$$Identifier \rightarrow \text{``}the\text{''}$$

$$Noun \rightarrow \text{``}Richard\text{''}$$

$$Verb \rightarrow \text{``}is\text{''}$$

$$Noun \rightarrow \text{``}Quaker\text{''}$$

$$Noun \rightarrow \text{``}pacifist\text{''}$$

Starting from S and using these production rules one can generate the correct sentences.

"Richard is a Quaker"
"The Quaker is a pacifist"

as well as the nonsensical.

"A Quaker is the Richard"

However our purpose at the moment is not to give a natural language generator rather it is to illustrate the origin of production systems.

In general therefor production systems will represent knowledge about the world in terms of condition action pairs. For example we might represent our some of our robot's knowledge using the following rules.

RULE 1 IF Robot is AT(Place-X)
  AND NOT BETWEEN(Place-X, Place-Y, Obstacle)
  THEN Can-Move-From-to(Robot, Place-X, Place-Y)
RULE 2 IF Robot is AT(Place-X)

AND Object-Y is AT(Place-X)

AND Graspable(Object-Y)

THEN Can-Pick-Up(Robot, Object-Y)

RULE 3 IF size(Object-Y) is less than 5 centimetres

AND weight(Object-Y) is less than 100 grams

THEN Graspable(Object-Y)

Given a production rule, such as one of those above, it is said to *fire* when all the conditions in its action part are true. The inference process associated to a production system can be set up in several ways. For the moment we content ourselves with the following description. At any moment in the evolution of the system a certain set of rules will have fired. Some of these will have been acted upon. Amongst those that have not been acted upon one is chosen and its action is invoked.

2.2.1 Characteristics of Rule-Based Systems

There are three principal things to note about the use of production systems for knowledge representation. The first is that they should be designed to facilitate pattern matching. That is to say that the condition part of the rule should be expressible in terms of a small number of concepts. More formally the language of the conditions will use the logical connectives AND, OR, NOT together with operators such as 'is' 'is less than' and a set of relations. This will make the translation of the rules into code straightforward. It also provides for an interface which is somewhat 'user friendly'.

Secondly we note that each rule is numbered. This serves a number of purposes. One is to allow the action part of one rule to invoke another rule. As we shall see when we discuss reasoning in production systems this allows for meta-rules that can control the progress of the system. Another use for this is that it permits the system to keep track of the rules that have fired so as to permit the system to explain its reasoning. The numbering of the rules also allows one to define a precedence order on the rules. Since it can happen that two rules fire at the same time it it is necessary to decide which rule will be chosen. Various methods are possible, but one is simply to choose the lowest numbered rule that has not yet been used.

Thirdly we note that a rule based system supports modularity in a natural way. This is both good and bad. Good because it suports modularity, bad because the control system can make it difficult to follow the effect of adding a new rule, particularly if its effect propagates outside the module in which it is added.

Rules can be added independently of the other rules, subject only to the provision that they do not introduce inconsistencies; a situation which can theoretically be verified. Furthermore by limiting the cross referencing between the rules and the relations that they consider it is possible to partition the knowledge base. This is clearly advantageous in the construction of large systems.

Fourthly, and related to the previous point, the existence of metarules means that there is a natural hierarchy that can be imposed on the rules themselves. In particular those rules that relate to the control of the system can be kept in one module.

Fifthly, one can incorporate uncertainty into a rule based system in a fairly natural way. Indeed this appears to have been one of the primary reasons for the choice of rules as knowledge representation method in MYCIN.

Sixth and lastly rules themselves have structure that allows one to structure the knowledge base. Recent work of John Debenham [32], [31] in this area shows that this can be a powerful technique.

2.2.2   Structuring Knowledge Bases

The theory of databases has benefited greatly from the introduction of the relational model. One of the ways in which this has manifested itself is in the use of functional dependencies to decompose the universal relation into smaller relations from which the original information can all be recovered. The work of John Debenham goes some way towards doing the same thing for knowledge bases. For the purposes of the discussion to follow we adopt the following definition of a knowledge base.

Definition 2.2.1 *A Knowledge Base (L,R,T,F,C,V) consists of*

1. *V is a set of Variables;*

2. *C is a set of constants;*

3. *F is a set of functions;*

4. *T is a set of relations;*

5. *L is a language built from (T,F,C,V) using the logical connectives AND, OR, and NOT;*

6. *R is a set of rules of the form IF condition THEN action, where both condition and action are statements from the language L.*

The rules thus impose additional structure upon the knowledge base that takes the statements of first order language and distinguishes those that require the use of the IF – THEN structure from those built up using the logical connectives. The quantifiers $\forall$ and $\exists$ are excluded from the language while the symbol $\rightarrow$ achieves a special status in that statements that include it are called rules.

Suppose now that we consider an example in which we concentrate upon a relation called *store* describing the storage location of some item. We might have the following rules
IF perishable(X) AND thawed(X) THEN store(X, refrigerator).
IF perishable(X) AND frozen(X) THEN store(X, freezer).
IF canned(X) THEN store(X, pantry).
Following Debenham it is possible to represent this collection of rules graphically as follows.

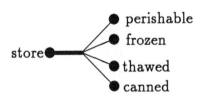

Debenham calls this a *dependencies diagram* for the rule. The name is deliberately reminiscent of functional dependency in database theory. The use of the thickened line conveys the coming together of the predicates. A knowledge base can be represented by a collection of these dependency diagrams. This collection of diagrams is called the combined diagram. A typical combined diagram is shown below.

The diagrams allow one to resolve a number of problems relevant to
the knowledge representation enterprise.

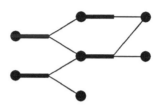

Inference proceeds from right to left. Debenham calls the nodes
at the far left query nodes and those at the right (that is to say those
having no thick lines emanating from them) as update nodes.

Minimal Rule Sets

Definition 2.2.2 *The rule set R of a knowledge base is* minimal *if
removing a rule from the knowledge base disconnects a query node
from the combined dependency graph.*

Note that minimality says nothing about consistency of the rules.
It is defined purely combinatorially.

Normalization of Rule Sets

Closely related to the topic of minimal rule sets is the topic of dependencies between rules. Just as the functional dependencies in a
database describe how the various attributes of a relation are connected and thus require the attributes to be kept together for update
purposes so there will be sets of rules that are inter-related. It is not
possible to give a detailed description of the process of normalizing
a knowledge base here; the interested reader should refer to Debenham's book [32]. However the topic is of sufficient relevance that a
brief description giving the flavour is justified.

I will give two examples of normalization, using the dependency
diagrams to illustrate the ideas. For the first example consider the
combined diagram.

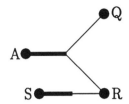

This diagram represents the combination of two rules.

RULE-A. IF Q AND R THEN A

RULE-B. IF R THEN S

RULE-A should be replaced by

RULE-*A'*. IF Q and S THEN A

which gives the combined diagram.

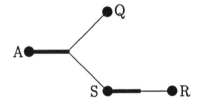

This normalization has a parallel in the GENERALIZE routine in the learning algorithm given by Ranan Banerji in [5]. Pictorially what is happening is that the point of attachment of the diagram for RULE-B is pushed back as far as possible.

The second normalization argument is similar. Given a diagram of the form:

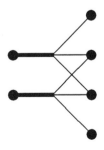

It can be replaced by one that appears as follows.

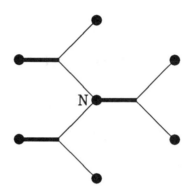

The node labeled N is a new relation implied by the common part of the two original rules. This parallels the DREAM procedure in the previously cited paper of Banerji [5]. Note once again the need to pull back the attachment point as far as possible.

In each of these cases it is possible to write an algorithm that will search through the rules looking for instances of the diagrams that can be modified. For details the reader is referred to [32]. What is of interest to us here is the fact that the pictures suggest ways of restructuring the knowledge base. An example of representation suggesting language and thence algorithm.

Minimal Storage for Knowledge Bases

The combined dependency diagram allows one to pose the following question. Assume that we are content to ask the questions posed by the query nodes. What is the minimal amount of information that we need to maintain in order to be able to answer these questions? Let us call a relation whose value is to be kept a *stored* relation. Then what we want to have happen is that

- All the values in the stored relation can be deduced from the values in the update relations, and

- all the values in the query relations can be deduced from the values in the stored relations.

I shall not go into great detail here, (the interested reader is referred to [31] for details.

Definition 2.2.3 *A* storage allocation *is a subset of the set of nodes in the combined diagram of a knowledge base such that if the subset is removed the diagram would consist of two connected, possibly empty, components with one component containing no query nodes and the other no update nodes.*

An irreducible storage allocation *is one for which the removal of a single node causes it to cease to be a storage allocation.*

A storage allocation is a division *if it contains no two nodes that depend upon one another.*

If each relation has an associated storage cost then graph theoretical algorithms can be used to find the minimal cost division and the minimal storage allocation [31].

Two observations on this work are of particular relevance to us here. The first is that the introduction of a particular graphical representation of the knowledge has suggested in a very immediate way methods for solving problems of real interest in the knowledge representation field. Secondly we observe that none of this relates specifically to the inference method used in the knowledge base.

2.3   Semantic Networks

There is an old psychological and pedagogic trick in which the subject is asked to pronounce a sequence of words which are spelled out to her. One such sequence might be

MacDuff, Macbeth, MacDonald, MacInnes, MacHine.

When the trick works the subject pronounces the last word as 'MacHine' , as my deliberately incorrect orthography suggests, rather than in the more normal way 'mach-ine' , as in 'machine intelligence'. This trick, and a number of others like it, suggest that human knowledge is stored in a form that keeps related concepts close together. If this is the case the activation of one set of concepts will bias the interpretation of new evidence in the direction of fitting it into the current context. Semantic networks provide one way of organizing knowledge that will incorporate this kind of bias. The use of the word bias is perhaps unfortunate since there is nothing necessarily undesirable about this kind of conditioning of the interpretation of evidence based upon the current context. Admittedly there will be occasions, as in the example above, where the wrong conclusion will be drawn, but it is a powerful means for narrowing search.

Semantic Nets have a long history as a knowledge representation tool. Partly as a consequence of this there are many things that have been called semantic networks. (Indeed there have even been suggestions that the term has outlived its usefulness and should no longer be used.) The reader can get some idea of the diversity of the family of semantic networks by reading the papers on the topic that are reproduced in Brachman and Levesque's book [16]. In my discussion of semantic networks I will concentrate on three types of networks that seem to me to exemplify the several different approaches. In order to introduce them we need first to give a definition of semantic network that is general enough to cover all the examples. The resulting concept is so general that it already exists without the adjective semantic.

Definition 2.3.1 *A* network *is an ordered pair* $(\mathcal{N}, \mathcal{L})$. *The elements of* $\mathcal{N}$ *are called the* nodes *of the network and the elements of* $\mathcal{L}$ *are called the* links *of the network. Each node is labeled. Each link is associated to an ordered pair of distinct nodes called its end-points.*

A network is thus just a directed graph, with labeled nodes. The three types of semantic networks that we will discuss can be distinguished as follows.

1. Semantic networks in which the links are labeled. I call these **IS-A** networks.

2. Semantic Networks in which the nodes can be divided into two sets. *Concept* nodes and *Relation* nodes. Following Sowa [91] I call these conceptual graphs.

3. Semantic Networks in which the attachment points of the links are part of the node label. I call these frame networks.

Each of these types of network has its own special characteristics which I will discuss in the following subsections.

2.3.1 IS-A Networks

IS-A networks carry the semantics of the representation on their links. The reason for calling them IS-A networks can be seen in the following well-known example.

Even this very simple IS-A network has some subtleties that need to be pointed out. First it is important to note that not all the nodes are of the same type, in spite of their being depicted as though they were. In this case the node labeled 'Clyde' is an *instance node*. That is to say that it denotes a specific object in the universe, whereas the two other nodes are *concept nodes*; in this case the concepts are 'elephant' and 'mammal'. Thus IS-A is here being used in two senses. The link on the left denotes class membership, Clyde is a member of the class elephant, whereas the link on the right is more properly a subset inclusion: all elephants are mammals.

Lest the reader assume that 'IS-A' is the only label that a link can have we give another example of an IS-A network on which there are links of different types.

Here the node labels that have numbers in them indicate that this is an instance node. The network represents the statement

block1 rests on the top of table1.

One property that IS-A networks share with all network representations is that the network has knowledge implicit in its structure. With appropriate choice of links IS-A networks can represent complex semantics. One way in which this can be done is through the use of *prototypes*. We can illustrate this in the context of our earlier example of the block resting on a table. If we remove the instance

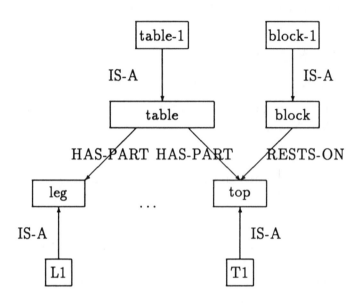

nodes from the network we get a template which represents the concept of a block resting on a table, rather than the specific instance of *block* − 1 resting on *table* − 1. This prototype, which is diagrammed below, allows us to infer that a table has a top and legs, and that the block rests on the top not on the legs.

This use of networks to provide prototypes is the basis of the *schema* approach. This was described by Schank and Abelson in their

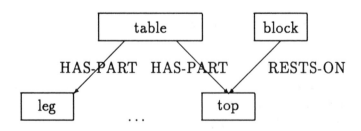

work on scripts [88]. We will give a formal definition of schema in the next subsection, for the moment it is enough to think of a schema as an IS-A network in which there are no instantiated instance nodes. Some special uninstantiated nodes may be necessary to connect various parts of the schema together. Thus the schema that describes moving an object from one place to another must indicate that the same object is referred to on both cases although no specific object has to be instantiated to do this.

A script is a sequence of schema that tell a story, the traditional one is the 'restaurant script'. The existence of a script allows the system to fill in missing details, such as for example that tables have legs, or that it is usual to pay for the meal at a restaurant.

While the capabilities of IS-A networks are impressive they have the potential drawback that the existence of a large number of possible link labels makes choosing the right link to follow a computational problem. Furthermore the potential for many different node types can also cause problems. Of course these potentialities contribute to the flexibility of IS-A networks.

2.3.2 Conceptual Graphs

Conceptual graphs as a form of semantic network were introduced by Sowa in [91]. Sowa makes an important distinction between conceptual graphs and the underlying semantic network. Conceptual graphs assert single propositions. They acquire meaning through their links to 'the semantic network'. Important though it is I shall not be further concerned with this distinction. Rather I want to show how conceptual graphs can serve to represent knowledge about the state of a system.

Where conceptual graphs differ from IS-A networks is that the links are unlabeled and there are two distinct types of nodes.

- Concept nodes, Objects such as Quaker, Cat, Block, and more sophisticated concepts such as sit, give, believe in;

- Relation nodes, which indicate how the concept nodes are related.

As a simple example we might consider a sentence involving a single transitive verb.

Johnny hit James.

This is to be represented as a conceptual graph in the following way

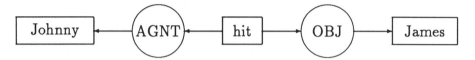

This box and circle notation is called the *display form* for the conceptual graph. Boxes are used to denote concept nodes and circles for relation nodes. There is also a form using brackets and parentheses that is more amenable to the linear output form that one is used to with computers. The example above can be written in this form as

$$[Johnny] \leftarrow (AGNT) \leftarrow [HIT] \rightarrow (OBJ) \rightarrow [James].$$

Propositions involving self reference mean that not every conceptual graph is linear. Special techniques are required to represent these in the above form. Sowa gives an example in his book [91].

A major difficulty that arises with formal knowledge representations is that without some additional restrictions the system permits the generation of objects that are meaningless. The simple minded grammar given earlier provides several examples of this. One of the virtues of Sowa's approach is that he is able to address this problem. The idea is to use a small number of "canonical" graphs from which all the needed ones can be constructed.

Sowa bases his construction of the "canon" on the notion of a type hierarchy. This is the underlying semantic network which about which the conceptual graphs make assertions. There is a function *type* which maps concepts into a set T whose elements are type labels. This function corresponds to the IS-A arcs that we encountered earlier in the first example of semantic nets. It is assumed that there is a type hierarchy which is a partial ordering of the type labels. In a conceptual graph individual concepts can have individual markers. Distinct markers attached to the same type label will then represent different instances of the same concept. This is the distinction between types and tokens. Following Sowa we use the notation $t :: i$ to indicate that the individual marker i is related to the type t. i is called the referent of the concept t. There is a generic referent $*$, used for generic instances.

Canonical graphs are based upon the notion of a conformity relation.

Definition 2.3.2 *Let T be a set of all type labels , and let I be a set of all individual markers. The conformity relation $::$ is defined on $T \times I$ so that*

1. *The referent of a concept must conform to its type label: if c is a concept $type(c) :: referent(c)$.*

2. *If an individual marker conforms to a type s it must conform to all supertypes of s in the type hierarchy.*

3. *If an individual type conforms to two types s and t then it must conform to their maximal common subtype.*

4. *Every individual marker conforms to the universal type $\top$; no individual marker corresponds to the absurd type $\bot$.*

5. *The generic marker conforms to all type labels.*

Evidently the type hierarchy is required to form a lattice. We can now define the basis for canonical graphs.

Definition 2.3.3 *The canon is a quadruple $(T, I, ::, B)$ where*

- *T is a type hierarchy.*

- *I is a set of individual makers.*

- *$::$ is a conformity relation between the labels of T and the markers I.*

- *B is a finite set of conceptual graphs called the canonical basis, with all type labels in T and all referents either in I or equal to $*$.*

The canonical graphs are those that can be formed from the canon by the rules of inference. We shall discuss these in detail in the next chapter. In summary they are as follows.

Definition 2.3.4 *The four canonical formulation rules for deriving a conceptual graph w from conceptual graphs u and v are*

1. Copy. *An exact copy w can be made u*

2. Restrict. *For any concept c in u, type(c) can be replaced by a subtype; if c is generic its referent can be changed to an individual marker. Such a change is permitted only if the referent of c conforms to type(c) before and after the change.*

3. Join. *If a concept c in u is identical to a concept d in v, then w is the graph obtained by identifying c and d in the union of u and v.*

4. Simplify. *If the conceptual relations r and s in a graph u are duplicates, then one of them can be deleted from u together with all its arcs.*

The canon will contain graphs such as:

$$[SLEEP] \leftarrow (AGNT) \leftarrow [ANIMAL]$$

and

$$[ROBOT] \leftarrow (AGNT) \leftarrow [CARRIES] \rightarrow (OBJ) \rightarrow [BLOCK]$$

this will forbid such statements as "Dreams sleep" but not "The robot carries a one ton weight". The aim is to prevent the formation of gibberish, ungrammatical statements, and statements that violate selectional constraints. The formation of counterfactual statements is not forbidden. Nor indeed is it desirable to do so, since learning programs must be able to consider hypotheses that are plausible even if in fact they are false.

There is one more aspect of Sowa's work which we must touch on before we turn to the next topic. Since conceptual graphs are supposed to represent statements about the world it should be possible to use logic to make the same statements. That is exactly the content of the following.

Proposition 2.3.5 *There is an operator ϕ mapping conceptual graphs into formulas in the first-order predicate calculus.*

Proof. Let u be any conceptual graph, then ϕu is the formula determined as follows.

1. For each generic concept c_i in u assign a distinct variable symbol x_i, $i = 1 \dots k$.

2. For each concept c assign a monadic predicate whose name is the same as $type(c)$ and whose argument is $identifier(c)$.

3. For each $n - adic$ conceptual relation r of u assign an $n - adic$ predicate whose name is the same as $type(r)$. For each i $\epsilon 1 \dots n$ let the ith argument of the predicate be the identifier of the concept linked to the ith arc of r.

4. ϕu has the quantifier prefix $\exists x_1 \exists x_2 \dots \exists x_k$ and a body consisting of the conjunction of all the predicates for the concepts and the conceptual relations of u.

□

Conceptual graphs provide a rich methodology for structuring knowledge, particularly as it is related to the question of natural language processing. The canon serves as a way to reduce the kinds of statements that can be formed to those that are likely to be reasonable.

2.3.3 Frame Networks

The final kind of network that I want to discuss is one where the arcs are labeled at their end-points. If we consider the statement

The robot carries the block.

then this kind of network would represent the statement as is depicted in the following diagram.

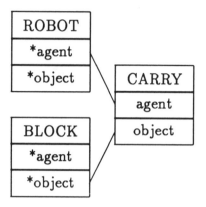

In this example the labels on the nodes are given by the upper case symbols, ROBOT, BLOCK and CARRY, whereas the labels for the links are in lower case. It is to be noted that every link is between a pair of labels of the form (label, *label). This gives a direction to the link. The type of a node is determined by the link labels that are present. Thus a node that has an *agent link and an object link represents a verb.

Frame networks were first introduced by S.C. Shapiro [89], though he did not use the name that I have chosen for them. The major benefit that is conferred by using frame networks is the elimination of the problem of typing the links. On the other hand each node has to have a type, which in turn determines the links that can originate form the node.

Perhaps more important is the fact that frame networks enforce a separation between the conceptual level of the network which relates to the items that are represented and the system level which gives the structural interconnections and bindings of the concepts. Thus by making each node have slots for the links that may be attached to it one has in some measure defined the semantics of the concept. For example the robot introduced above is allowed to be either agent or object. The links that are present in a particular network determine which role the robot is playing and with respect to which concepts it plays that role.

2.3.4 Representing Knowledge in Semantic Networks

We would like to be able to formalize the sense in which a semantic network represents the world. One way in which we could do this is by using logic as an intermediary. If we were to go this way we would argue that since there is a translation from a semantic net representation to logic, for example we could use Sowa's function ϕ defined in proposition 2.3.5, and since there are formal world models for logic we can thus obtains a formal model of the representation corresponding to a semantic network. While from some points of view (existence for example) this might be perfectly adequate it ignores the fact that semantic networks attempt to capture more than just logical propositions. They also model the associations between concepts. Any formalization of the model that a network creates should acknowledge this.

To some extent a semantic network already carries its own model. The IS-A links that are instance links and the referents of Sowa's conceptual graphs provide a map to specific objects. It seems reasonable therefor to regard the model of a semantic network as a graph, just as we did at the beginning of the section. More formally

Definition 2.3.6 *A Semantic network is a graph* $G = (\mathcal{N}, \mathcal{L})$, *whose node* $\mathcal{N}$ *are the objects of the network and whose arcs* $\mathcal{L}$ *are the links of the network.*

There are the following network types

- IS-A networks *in which the links are labeled.*

- Conceptual Graphs *in which the nodes are divided into two sets, concepts and relations and every link joins a concept to a relation. Conceptual graphs are thus bipartite graphs.*

- Frame Networks *in which there is a finite list of attachment types,* $\mathcal{A} = ((a), \ldots, (n))$. *Each node* $n \epsilon \mathcal{N}$ *is labeled with a bag* type(n) *of types whose elements are either attachment types* k *or dual attachment types* $*k$. *The elements of this bag are called the attachment points of the node. Each link in the graph joins* *a pair of attachment points* $(n_1, k), (n_2, *k)$ *whose attachment types are dual to one another.*

The graphs themselves should be considered as the formal models, with as we shell see the formal methods of manipulating semantics networks deriving from their graphical representation.

2.4   Frames

The subject of frames has been somewhat anticipated in out discussion of frame networks. Indeed frame based knowledge representation owes much to semantic networks. There is a sense in which the relationship between frames and semantic networks is similar to the relationship between the hierachical and network models of a database. Many frame based systems insist on a hierarchical organization for the frames whereas in a semantic network there is no requirement that the nodes form a hierarchy.

However frames have come to have a much richer structure than the nodes of semantic networks, even frame networks were originally conceived as having. However before we discuss frames in detail it is appropriate to introduce attribute value pairs.

2.4.1   Objects, Attributes, and Values

Attribute value pairs have been used for knowledge representation since the earliest days. Lisp provides specific support for the notion. Objects have property lists which are lists of < *attribute, value*> pairs. Thus Richard might have the property list:

(<Religion, Quaker>, <Party-affiliation, Republican>).

Property lists thus become a way to encapsulate information about an object with the object itself. The pair (Object, Attribute-Value-List) is in essence the object itself. Just as the set of attachment labels is the type of an object in a frame network,so the nature of an object is determined by its attribute-value list.

More significant for knowledge representation however is the possibility of attaching functions as the values of an attribute. Thus the

property list for a Robot might have attributes that are functions
that move the robot. In this way not only does one have information
about such things as size and shape of the object stored with it but
also information about how to manipulate the object as well.

Used by themselves attribute value lists can lead to enormous
duplication of information. Thus the property list for Richard will
contain a great deal of information that is specific to Richard and
much more that is related to the fact that Richard is a human being.
Frame based knowledge representations borrow from IS-A networks
an inheritance structure which avoids this reduplication of information.

2.4.2   Frame Hierarchies

Definition 2.4.1 *A frame $\mathcal{F}$ is an attribute value list (S, V). Each
S is called a slot of the frame. The value V of a slot may be either*

- *A value, whose type is determined by the slot, or a function
  returning a value of that type.*

- *An attribute value list, where the attributes are boolean functions
  and the values are either functions returning values of the slot
  value type or constants of the slot value type.*

It is appropriate at this point to remark on the relationship between this use of the word frame and the use in the context of the
"frame problem". Suppose that one has some representation of the
world. For example the world of a robot in a room with a number of
coloured objects. Suppose that the robot moves, how does the robot
"know" that the objects do not change colour?. For Minsky [71] a
frame is a structure that one selects from memory to be adapted to
reality by changing details as necesary. Thus as the robot moves some
details must be changed and others not. This kind of frame is related
to the definition above in that one has one large frame with slots describing the objects and their properties and it is the values in this
frame of reference that may change.

In order to solve the information repetition problem the world is
to be represented by a hierachy of frames, where the links are all IS-A

links. These links are specific slots in the frame. Furthermore slots
and their values are inherited along these links.

As in the case of IS-A networks the IS-A links have a slightly
ambiguous connotation since they can mean different things in different circumstances. For example there will be an IS-A link from
a Kitchen frame to a room frame, along which the kitchen will inherit such things as doors, walls, a floor and a ceiling. Here the IS-A
link means that Kitchen is a subclass of room, whereas a specific instance of a kitchen will inherit slots for a stove and sink from the
class kitchen. In this case the IS-A link plays the role of instantiat-
ing an object in the kitchen class. So the IS-A links indicate both
membership and subset.

We can give a formal definition of a frame hierarchy as follows.

Definition 2.4.2 *A frame hierarchy is a tree each of whose nodes
is a frame. For each child node the link to the parent node is an*
inheritance link. *The child node inherits all the slots of its parent
unless they are specifically overidden in the child. In addition nodes
can be of two kinds: class nodes and instance nodes. An internal node
of the tree must be a class node.*

In order to be give a semantic interpretation for a frame hierarchy
we will work in two stages. We first give an interpretation of a frame,
and then fit the interpretations of individual frames together.

Since a frame is to represent either an individual or a class it seems
reasonable to try for a set theoretical interpretation. Suppose that
we have a universe U of and a collection $\mathcal{A}$ of partial functions on $\mathcal{U}$.
These partial functions are the attributes. The range of an attribute
is the value set of the attribute, and may be itself a function of some
kind. Then the pair $(\mathcal{U}, \mathcal{A})$ is a model for a frame F if the attributes
in F can be mapped to the attribute set $\mathcal{A}$ so that the values of the
attributes of F are mapped to the values of the image attributes in
$\mathcal{A}$. This map will be called the attribute representation map. Thus
each frame is represented as a set of possible maps. Each possible
map being defined by its domain and range. It can of course happen
that the value of one of the attributes is completely defined in which
case the range is a singleton set. (We shall see later that the Cyc

system adopts the convention that values of this kind are represented by singleton sets, essentially for exactly this reason.)

In the above we have not considered the possibility of inheritance links. Suppose that we have two frames F_1, and F_2 such that the attributes in the image of the attribute representation map for F_1 are a subset of the attributes in the image of F_2 and that the corresponding values are equal. In this case we say that F_2 inherits the attributes of F_1 or rather that F_2 IS-A F_1. The attribute list of F_2 can then be given by a reference to the attribute list of F_1 and the list of additional attributes.

2.5 The Formal Concept of A Knowledge base

To conclude this chapter I will review the unifying concepts that seem to underly all the different knowledge representation methods. Informally we may construe a knowledge base as being a way of storing useful information about the world in a way that is suited to inference. A knowledge base thus does not store all its information explicitly some is stored implicitly.

A knowledge base relates to a specific "universe" U of objects. In a specific knowledge representation there are two ways in which objects are identified. They can be identified by reference as "block-001' or by the use of the knowledge representation language to give identifying properties. For example in the case of logical representation, block-001 could be defined by giving a list of predicates that it must satisfy, such as ON(Table, Block), Colour(Block, Red). In the frame representation the same block might be specified by giving the value of the attributes position and colour, where both of these attributes could be inherited from the universal object.

Formally we have

Definition 2.5.1 *A* Knowledge Representation System *for a universe U consists of*

1. *a collection L of labels that can represent individuals in the universe, These labels are divided into constants and variables.*

2. *a collection $\mathcal{F}$ of functions,*

3. *a collection $\mathcal{R}$ of relations,*

4. *a language $\mathcal{L}$ consisting of rules for combining the functions, relations and labels into well formed expressions of the language,*

5. *a semantics S that gives meaning to the labels, functions and relations.*

The Knowledge representation language supports a method for specifying individuals or classes of individuals in terms of the functions and relations. This may be logical or functional.

The presence of item 5 in the above definition is the most important aspect of any knowledge representation system [72]. There are several ways in which the semantics can be determined. Of these mapping the system into the set of subsets of some universal set provides the commonest model. However as we have seen it is possible to provide other models. Debenham's mapping of rule sets onto dependency diagrams is one such example.

In general one would expect a knowledge base to support operations **tell** and **ask** that allow thew user to use the knowledge base. By analogy with database a complete knowledge representation supports a knowledge query and assertion language.

The methods of knowledge representation that we have described are all designed to be somewhat universal in that there are to be used to describe a large part of the world that an intelligent agent must interact with. One possibility to which we shall return later is that in the case of much narrower domains one can represent knowledge by using much more structured systems. The use of the language of machines in the representation of problem solving is just one such example. This addition of structure is a powerful technique because it permits a reduction in the amount of search that is required. We shall return to this topic in subsequent chapters.

Finally we note that an important aspect of a knowledge base is that the information about individuals is not kept in explicit form for all the individuals in the universe. Rather there is a system for deducing information about an individual from other information. It is to this question of reasoning that we must now turn.

Chapter 3

Reasoning

This chapter will be concerned with the reasoning paradigms used in Artificial Intelligence. I will discuss the degree to which they are dependent upon a particular form of knowledge representation.

3.1 Search

Search has always been one of the primary techniques of reasoning in Artificial Intelligence. Typically one has a search space S, an initial position s_0 and a goal set G. In addition there is a set Ω of actions that allow one to move about the search space. The objective is to find a sequence of actions from Ω that will transform the current state into one that is in G.

This description has been deliberately left somewhat vague so as to apply to the many distinct situations that arise in AI. We shall see that the framework is in fact general enough to do this. Before proceeding with a detailed discussion of search methods there are a number of points that must be made.

The most important point to note is that at a given point in the state space only some of the actions in Ω may apply. Indeed some of the problem may lie in determining which actions do so. In a purely formal sense this can be overcome by renaming the actions so that there effect is the identity in places where they do not apply. However this discards what is in fact quite significant information about a particular move, namely the set of states to which it applies.

Indeed there are problem solving methods such as GPS [74] where this information is used in a critical way to find the solution.

A second point to note is that in real life not all the actions that can be taken are reversible. In the game Hi-Q (also called solitaire) when a piece has been hopped over it is removed from play, thus making it impossible to recover the position as it as before the move was made. While it is possible to backtrack in the search space the formal models that are often used for simplifying search in the cases where moves can be undone do not apply in these kinds of examples.

A third difficulty that often arises is the specification of the goal state. While for some kinds of problems, such as object placement, it may be possible to specify the goal in advance in a quite precise way, there are other problems where the goal is given in terms of a property that may not permit the easy construction of specific states that satisfy the property. Here again we have a case where some of the standard methods fail.

The default search algorithm is often referred to as the British Museum Algorithm after the notorious monkeys and their typewriters. A somewhat more dignified term for it is exhaustive search. As the name suggests the method involves systematically generating every state in the search space and then testing it to see if it is a goal state. It is clearly desirable to be able to reduce the size of the search as much as one can. Discussions of this problem form a large part of the AI literature [26] so I shall not be giving an comprehensive discussion of all the search reduction techniques here. I will concentrate on those that bear a close relation to the representation methods that were introduced in the last chapter.

To do this I want to divide search procedures into two types. The distinction is in some sense completely artificial since one can translate a search of one kind into a search of the other kind quite readily. It is however a useful classification which carries some real significance. I will call the two methods, graph searching and pattern searching. Graph searching models the search as being an attempt to find a path through a graph, whereas pattern searching uses pattern matching as the search paradigm.

3.1.1 Graph Searches

In a graph search we model the search space as a graph. The vertices of the graph correspond to the states and the edges correspond to the allowable transformations. Formally we have

Definition 3.1.1 *A search graph is a directed graph* $\mathcal{G} = (N, E)$ *with labelling* $\Lambda : E \to \Omega$, *start state a node* s_0 *in* N *and goal state a subset* G *of* N.

A path *in a search graph is a sequence* $n_0, \ldots n_k$ *of distinct nodes of* $\mathcal{G}$ *such that for each pair* (n_i, n_{i+1}) *of consecutive nodes in the sequence, there is an edge* e_i *of* $\mathcal{G}$ *going from* n_i *to* n_{i+1}.

A solution *in a search graph is a path* $n_0, \ldots n_k$ *such that* $n_0 = s_0$ *and* n_k *is a node in* G. *The corresponding sequence of edge labels will also be called a solution.*

In the above definition I intentionally introduced the notion of a path in the graph separately from the solution so as to be able to encompass three approaches to finding the solution. These are

- Forward Search. All paths are to begin at the start and are extended forwards until one of them contains a goal node.

- Backward Search. All paths are to end at a goal node and are extended backwards until one of them contains the start node.

- Opportunistic Search. Paths are extended on either end until one of them joins the start to a goal.

Two variations of the last technique are worth noting. Paths can be joined together to make longer ones, (the removal of duplicate nodes is straightforward.) Secondly one can combine a forward search and a backward search by looking for forward paths that meet backward ones. This latter method is due to DeChampeaux and Pohl [30]

It is important to understand that the graph may in fact not be given to one directly when one is searching. It is likely that one has a criterion for recognizing when one has reached a goal state and the list Ω of allowable transformations. Typically therefor during a graph search one has available the following information.

- A (possibly partial) description of the current state.

- A set of criteria for recognizing a goal state

- A finite set of actions some of which can be applied to the current state.

Search reduction requires that one find a way to restrict the number of choices that one has at any given state. Methods for doing this have fallen into two distinct classes. There are the variations of best first search and then there are methods that rely on some form of decomposition of the state space.

Best First Searches

In order to detail the notion of a best first search let us give a generic search algorithm. We use forward search as a model although the other searches fit the model.

Algorithm 3.1.2 *Suppose that we have a search graph. Then at any stage during the search we have the following:*

- *An agenda* OPEN *of nodes that have been generated but not yet explored, each node has attached to it a path between it and the start node.*

- *A list* CLOSED *of nodes that have been explored.*

WHILE OPEN *is not empty and no goal state has been found.*

1. *Remove some node n from* OPEN.

2. *If the node is a goal node exit with success otherwise   generate the states accessible from n. Add some or all of them to* OPEN *and move n to* CLOSED.

   If this point is reached the search has failed. Exit with failure.

The best first nature of the algorithm is inherent in the way that the node is chosen from OPEN. The decision not to place certain nodes onto OPEN is called pruning. A detailed description of best first algorithms and their inter-relationships is given by Pearl in his book "Heuristics" [79]. Generally best first algorithms do not in fact prune the search tree, however some nodes are viewed as so unpromising that they are always a long way down the agenda.

Production rule based knowledge representation fits very nicely into this framework. The rules represent preferred paths through the network. Forward and backward chaining correspond to the forward and backward searches while opportunistic searches match the blackboard approach which we will examine when we come to deal with large scale systems.

Search Space Decomposition

An alternative approach to search reduction can be based upon the idea of search space decomposition. Intuitively we can think of the search space as being broken up into subsets. The search then decomposes into first finding a sequence of subsets that join the one containing the start state to the one that contains the goal state and secondly working out how to traverse each subset.

There have been a number of descriptions of versions of this idea for example Banerji and Ernst [8] used it to describe GPS [74]. The work of Niizuma and Kitahashi [77] is another. I will give a general formalism that covers the thrust of most if not all the special cases.

Suppose therefor that we have a search graph S with start state s_0 and goal set G. Let R be an equivalence relation on the nodes of S. We can form a new graph S/R whose nodes are the equivalence classes of R. The edge set of S/R is the same as the edge set of S. Each edge in S/R joins the nodes in S/R that are the images of its end points in S. Each node in S/R that is the image of a goal node in S is a goal node in S/R.

Given a path on S joining the start state to a goal state we clearly have a corresponding path in S/R. What is not clear, indeed may not even be true, is that having a path on S/R allows us to deduce the existence of a path in S. In fact we now have two problems. The first is finding a path on S/R and the second is that of lifting this path to S. Note however that there is reason to believe that each of these two problems may be simpler than the original one. In the first place S/R is a smaller graph in that it has fewer nodes. Secondly the lifting problem reduces to finding paths on the equivalence classes, which are also smaller than the original graph.

We can clarify the foregoing somewhat by being more precise. Suppose that we have found a path $e_0 e_1 \ldots e_k$ on S/R. If we regard these edges as being edges of S rather than edges of S/R (which we can since each edge of S/R comes from an edge in S) then it will not necessarily be the case that the pairs $e_i e_{i+1}$ of adjacent edges in S/R continue to be adjacent in S. However since they are adjacent in S/R there is some node x in S such that e_i and e_{i+1} both meet the equivalence class $R(x)$. Let x_1 denote the terminal vertex of e_i and let x_2 denote the initial vertex of e_{i+1} then both x_1 and x_2 must belong to $R(x)$ and we have a search problem with domain $R(x)$, edges consisting of those edges of S both of whose vertices are in $R(x)$, start state x_1 and goal state x_2. Solution of each of these problems together with two special ones corresponding to the beginning and end of the chain on S/R will yield a solution to the original search problem.

In any practical application of this principle the major difficulty lies in finding an appropriate equivalence relation. If the names on the edge labels are not significant this is much simpler than when the names are important. This latter case occurs when the edges correspond to moves in some problem state and one wants to have the quotient graph also represent a set of moves on a problem space. Several workers have examined this problem in detail for example Paul Benjamin et al. [10] and the aforementioned work of Niizuma and Kitahashi [77] as well as work of myself [51].

3.1.2   Pattern Searches

The view of search presented in the previous subsection is the traditional geometric one suggested by the image of searching for the correct path through a labyrinth. I will now propose a somewhat different model for search. The model is more purely symbolic in nature, and is motivated by the idea of pattern matching. Intuitively one has two strings of symbols and a set of rules that allow one to replace one group of symbols by another. The goal is to find a sequence of symbol replacements that will transform the first string into the second.

A simple example of this kind of search is the game of word transformation. In this game one is given two words with the same number of letters, for example BOAT and WOOD, one must try to transform one word into the other one letter at a time, while preserving the property that at each step one has a word. In this case one the following is a solution.

$$\begin{array}{c} \text{BOAT} \\ \text{COAT} \\ \text{COAL} \\ \text{FOAL} \\ \text{FOOL} \\ \text{WOOL} \\ \text{WOOD} \end{array}$$

In spite of the almost trivial nature of this example it carries the basic idea of a pattern search quite explicitly. At each step there is a replacement of a substring of one string by a different string so as to form a new well formed string. We can capture this in the following way.

We suppose that a language L has been given. One can think of this as perhaps a language whose formulae are strings but they could also be graphs or any other construct that is appropriate. We need a notion of matching subformulae, which obtain as follows. We suppose that we are given

- a class of formula equivalences $f \cong g$ defined in the language,

- a notion of subformula $f \hookrightarrow g$.

Given this we say that two formulae p and q in L can be matched by the equivalence $f \cong g$ if

1. $f \hookrightarrow p$;

2. $g \hookrightarrow q$;

3. The formula equivalence $f \cong g$ extends to a transformation of p to q which is the identity outside the image of f in p.

Grammars determined by production rules provide a well-known example of this kind of approach. In fact production systems which are based upon the use of {*pattern, action*} pairs are typical of pattern searches. We also note that the rules of inference for conceptual graphs fall into this category. The use of this kind of equivalence in the case of graphs was first discussed by Ehrig in [36].

3.1.3   Searching and Knowledge Representation

Although we have already made some remarks earlier about the knowledge representation methods that match a particular search it is worthwhile to spend some more time on the topic.

We recall that we described four major classes of Knowledge Representation, logic, production systems, semantic networks, and frames. Let us briefly review the way in which each one fits with the search mechanisms.

Search in Logic

Most search in logic seems to be pattern directed. The rules of inference in logic when written in the form

$$\frac{Hypotheses}{Conclusion}$$

are presented in a form which is precisely one that specifies a pair of patterns, namely the hypotheses and the conclusion. Another example of this in its purest form is provided by Wang's algorithm.

Algorithm 3.1.3   *1. Write the proposition to be proved in the form*

$$A_1, A_2, \ldots A_n \to B$$

where the A_i are the hypotheses and B is the conclusion.

2. For each wff whose principal connective is a negation ($\sim$), drop the negation and move the wff to the other side of the arrow. The underlying equivalences here are

$$\sim A \to \ \Leftrightarrow \ \to A$$

and

$$\rightarrow \sim A \Leftrightarrow A \rightarrow$$

3. *If the principal connective on the left of an arrow is $\wedge$ or on the right is $\vee$ replace the connective by a comma. This corresponds to the equivalences*

$$A \wedge B \rightarrow C \Leftrightarrow A, B \rightarrow C \ and A \rightarrow B \vee C \Leftrightarrow A \rightarrow B, C$$

4. *If the principal connective on the left hand side is $\vee$ or on the right hand side is $\wedge$ then produce two new lines one containing each of the two sub-wffs replacing the original wff. This corresponds to*

$$(A \vee B \rightarrow C) \Leftrightarrow (A \rightarrow C); (B \rightarrow C)$$

and

$$(A \rightarrow B \vee C) \Leftrightarrow (A \rightarrow B); (A \rightarrow C)$$

All the lines separated by semicolons must be proved.

5. *If the same wff occurs on both sides of an arrow, the line is proven.*

6. *If no connectives remain and no propositional variable occurs on both sides of an arrow, the line is not provable.*

This algorithm shows quite nicely the basic methodology of a pattern search. In that it describes a series of pattern driven manipulations of a set of wffs.

Depending on how they are presented production systems can fall into either search category. The {*pattern, action*} presentation is a pattern search whereas if one adopts Debenham's view of rules as graphs as we did in our discussion of structuring of knowledge bases then one has a version of production systems that is more closely tied to the graph model of search.

Search in Networks

The very structure of a network would lead one to expect that the
preferred mode of search would be the graphical one. Indeed this is
the case most of the time. However the search method suggested by
Sowa for conceptual graphs is in fact a pattern search.

Frames provide an interesting example of a graph search since in
this case some needed information is not present at the node of current
interest. Thus the information that a kitchen has a floor, ceiling
and walls is not stored in the kitchen frame. However the explicit
hierachical structure of the frame network provides a preferred search
path for finding this information.

3.2   Logical Reasoning

Not surprisingly there is a long history of reasoning in logic. But is
is only in the twentieth century that much thought has been given
to the automation of reasoning. There is now a substantial literature
on automated reasoning, we should cite the work of Boyer and Moore
[14] as a landmark in this area. In view of this I will review the
methods of logical reasoning only briefly and with an eye to how they
fit into my context. I want to discuss two approaches deduction and
unification-resolution.

3.2.1   Deduction

Deduction is guided by a set of *rules of inference*. We met these first
when we introduced logic as a knowledge representation language.
Now we need to see how one could fit them into a framework for
deduction. A problem in deduction consists of the following (we will
not repeat here the rules for creating the formulae of first order logic.)

1. A collection H of wff's called the hypotheses.

2. A collection of deduction rules called the rules of inference.

3. A wff c that is to be proved, called the conclusion.

The process of deduction is a multi-step one in which at each stage a rule of inference can be used to deduce some intermediate conclusion. Thus at any stage in the process of deduction one has a set H_n of wffs each of which is either one of the original members of H or has been deduced from H. A single step consists of applying one of the rules R_n to obtain a conclusion c_{i+1} giving $H_{n+1} = H_n \cup c_{i+1}$. The deductive process succeeds when H_{n+1} contains c. The sequence of inferences that correspond to this process is called a *proof* of c from H.

In our description of first order logic we gave just two rules of inference, modus ponens and generalisation. There are many others that could be used. More important however is the idea of a subproof. This is parallel to the idea of a subroutine in a programming language. In fact this parallel is sufficiently important that it is worth making a digression to elaborate upon it.

Programs as Proofs

During the course of the deduction of a conclusion from a set of hypotheses it may happen that one uses essentially the same argument up to renaming of the variables that appear. For example a formal deduction that $\wedge$ is commutative (that is $p \wedge q = q \wedge p$), could proceed by showing that $p \wedge q \Rightarrow q \wedge p$ and then by reversing the roles of p and q that $q \wedge p \Rightarrow p \wedge q$.

Now one can think of a proof as a constructive process that transforms the hypotheses into the conclusion. So that to say that

$$H_1, H_2, \ldots H_n \text{ imply } C$$

means that there is some process P that transforms the H_i into C. If we now abstract away the precise values of the H_i then we can represent P in the λ-calculus formalism as $\Lambda x_1 \ldots x_n P$ and the 'evaluation' of P at $H_1, \ldots H_n$ is C.

$$\Lambda x_1 \ldots x_n P H_1 \ldots H_n = C$$

In this way a proof can be regarded as a formal language element and rules for manipulating proofs in the the way that other language elements are manipulated can be introduced into the formalism.

Note that this is in fact similar to the case of the graph search where we can use the traversal of a known subgraph as a single move. Thus we can recast the decomposition method in terms of subproofs. One case where this is transparent is the case of proving a conjunction.

$$H \Rightarrow C_1 \wedge C_2$$

If we consider the formal proof theoretic approach then we have the rule that tells us that

$$\frac{H \wedge \Lambda x P_1 H = C_1 \wedge \Lambda x P_2 = C_2}{C_1 \wedge C_2}$$

On the other hand if we take the graph view then the path that we want can be found by first seeking the goal of making C_1 true and then following it with one that makes C_2 true.

Other Inference Rules

So far we have only considered two rules of inference 'modus ponens' and generalisation. I want to list some others here and consider how they can by incorporated into a reasoning scheme. The list is not exhaustive, rather it is used to illustrate the ideas.

And elimination $\wedge - E$ allows one to replace a conjunction by any of its conjuncts.

$$\wedge - E : \frac{E_1 \wedge \ldots \wedge E_n}{E_i}$$

And insertion $\wedge - I$ allows one to asserts a conjunction when one believes each of the components.

$$\wedge - I : \frac{E_1, \ldots E_n}{E_1 \wedge \ldots \wedge E_n}$$

Or elimination

$$\vee - E : \frac{E_1 \vee \ldots \vee E_n, E_1 \Leftarrow E, \ldots E_n \Leftarrow E}{E}$$

Or Insertion

$$\vee - I : \frac{E_i}{E_1 \vee \ldots \vee E_n}$$

One interesting rule is the rule for eliminating existential quantifiers. This rule is called existential instantiation. Intuitively it says that if a sentence which is existentially quantified is true then there must be some instance of the variables that makes it true, so that we can deduce that instance.

Existential Instantiation

$$\exists - E : \frac{\exists x f(x)}{f(c)}$$

where c is a constant.

Since each of these rules is based upon replacing one pattern, namely that appearing above the line, with another — that occurring below the line, one can build an inference system based upon these rules of inference and a pattern search. The efficiency of the system is dependent upon several factors. Most important is the fact that if we allow rules that both insert and delete patterns then we do not have a guarantee that as the deduction process continues we are getting nearer to our goal. Thus just as in search procedures we must rely upon heuristic methods to choose the appropriate direction to go in at any point in the search.

3.2.2 Unification and Resolution.

If deduction proceeds by trying to transform the hypotheses into the conclusion, resolution works by trying to transform a collection of statements into the empty statement. Informally the idea is that one works by trying to satisfy a collection of statements. If one can reduce this to satisfying the empty statement one is done.

Resolution models of reasoning work with statements in *clausal form*. This is a simplified form of first order logic. The building blocks are *literals* which are atomic sentences (sometimes called *terms*). A literal which is the negation of an atomic sentence is called a negative literal. *Clauses* are sets of literals representing the disjunction of the component literals. Thus {**party-affiliation(X, Republican)**, **religion(X, Quaker)**} is a clause.

Reduction to Clausal Form

This restriction to clauses is not as limiting as might at first appear. The following algorithm show how a sentence in first order logic can be put into clausal form.

Algorithm 3.2.1   *1. Eliminate all occurrences of $\Leftarrow$ and $\Leftrightarrow$ by substituting equivalent sentence using only $\wedge$, $\vee$, $\sim$.*

- *$p \Leftarrow q$ is replaced by $\sim p \vee q$*
- *$p \Leftrightarrow q$ is replaced by $(\sim p \vee q) \wedge (\sim q \vee p)$.*

2. Distribute all negations $\sim$ over the other logical operators. (This will incidentally remove all double negations).

3. Rename all the variables so that each quantifier refers to a unique variable.

4. Remove all existential quantifiers. This proces is called Skolemisation and works as follows. Suppose we have the expression $\forall x \exists y p(x, y)$. This in fact asserts some kind of relation between y and x, namely that for all x there is some y that makes $p(x, y)$ true. We can imagine that the truth of this statement is vouchsafed by an oracle that produces the required y when we give it an x. In other words there is some function $f(x)$ giving the required y. Hence we can replace $\forall x \exists y p(x, y)$ by $\forall x p(x, f(y))$ where f is a function name distinct from any that may already appear.

5. Drop all universal quantifiers. Since all the variables are universally quantified this introduces no ambiguity.

6. Put the expression in conjunctive normal form, by distributing $\vee$ over $\wedge$.

7. Eliminate the operators $\vee$ and $\wedge$ by replacing $\vee$ by ',' and making each conjunct into a clause set. Thus $P \wedge (Q \vee R)$ is replaced by the two clause sets $\{P\}, \{Q, R\}$.

8. Rename the variables once more so that no variable name appears in more than one clause.

The resolution principle is most easily understood when no variables are present. So I will introduce it here before the introduction of unification.

Given a clause Φ containing a literal ϕ and another clause Ψ containing the literal $\sim \phi$ we can infer the clause $(\Phi \setminus \{\phi\}) \cup (\Psi \setminus \{\sim \phi\})$.

There is in fact nothing particularly mysterious about this. It is in fact a version of 'modus ponens'. Recall that modus ponens tells us that from $p \Leftarrow q$ and p we can infer q. If we start with $(p \Leftarrow q) \wedge p$ and apply the algorithm to reduce it to clausal form we get the two clauses $\{\sim p, q\}$ and $\{p\}$. Since the first clause contains $\sim p$ and the second contains p we can resolve to get q, which is, as claimed, exactly what modus ponens yields.

Unification

In order to be able to apply the resolution principle to clauses that contain variables we need some way of saying that a suitable choice of variables will identify two literals, (or more accurately one literal to the negation of another.) To make sense of this idea we need to introduce the notion of a substitution.

Definition 3.2.2 *A substitution θ is a finite set of pairs of the form $(X_i \mid E_i)$ where X_i is a variable and E_i is an expression. Furthermore $X_i \neq X_j$ for every $i \neq j$ and X_i does not occur in E_j for any i and j. Given a literal $P(X_1, \ldots X_n)$ we write $P(X_1 \mid E_1, \ldots, X_n \mid E_n)$ for the literal obtained by substituting the E_i for the corresponding X_i in P. For brevity we can write $P(X_1\theta, \ldots X_n\theta)$ or even $P\theta$.*

Unification deals with the idea of finding a substitution that makes two expressions or literals equal. More formally we have

Definition 3.2.3 *A set of expressions $\{p_1, \ldots p_n\}$ is unifiable if and only if there exists a substitution θ that makes the expressions identical that is $p_1\theta = \ldots = p_n\theta$. The substitution θ is called the unifier for the set.*

Given two expressions p and q there may be more than one way of unifying them. Suppose that the substitutions θ and σ both unify p

and q, we say that θ is more general than σ if there is a substitution δ such that $p\theta\delta = p\sigma = q\sigma$. In particular θ is called the *most general unifier* (mgu) for p and q if for any unifier σ of p and q it is the case that there is a substitution δ for which $p\theta\delta = p\sigma = q\sigma$. The following algorithm (taken from Sterling and Shapiro [92]) delivers the mgu of two expressions.

Algorithm 3.2.4 *To unify two expressions T_1 and T_2.*

1. *Initialise the substitution θ to be empty, the stack to contain the equation $T_1 = T_2$, and failure to false.*

2. **while** *the stack is not empty and no failure do*

   pop $X = Y$ from the stack

   case

   > X *is a variable which does not appear in Y:*
   > > *substitute Y for X in the stack*
   > > *and in θ add $X = Y$ to θ.*
   >
   > Y *is a variable that does not occur in X:*
   > > *substitute X for Y in the stack*
   > > *and in θ add $Y = X$ to θ.*
   >
   > X *and Y are identical constants or variables:*
   > > *continue*
   >
   > X *is $f(X_1, \ldots, X_n)$ and Y is $f(Y_1, \ldots, Y_n)$ for some functor f and $n \geq 1$:*
   > > *push $X_i = Y_i, i = 1, \ldots n$ on the stack*
   >
   > *otherwise:*
   > > *failure := true*

3. *if failure then output failure;*
   else output θ

We are now in a position to be able to complete the description of the resolution principle. Intuitively the idea is that we can perform resolution whenever we can find a unification between a pair of literals drawn from the two clauses. There is however one additional complication that is required. Suppose we are given a clause Φ and that some subset of the literals in Φ has a most general unifier, then the cluase Φ' obtained by applying the substitution associated to this unification is called a *factor* of Φ.

Definition 3.2.5 *The* resolution principle. *Suppose that Φ and Psi are two clauses. If there is a literal ϕ in some factor Φ' of Φ and a literal $\sim \psi$ in some factor Ψ' of Ψ such that ϕ and ψ have a most general unifier γ, then we say that Φ and Ψ resolve and that the clause*

$$((\Phi' \setminus \{\phi\}) \cup (\Psi' \setminus \{\sim \psi\}))\gamma$$

is a resolvent *of the two clauses.*

A *resolution deduction* of a clause Φ from a database Δ is a sequence of clauses in which

1. Φ is an element of the sequence, and

2. each element is either a member of Δ or the result of applying the resolution principle to clauses earlier in the sequence.

One of the most effective uses of resolution is in demonstating unsatisfiability. If a set of clauses cannot be satisfied then it is possible to use resolution to derive a contradiction. But in clausal form a contradiction is just the empty clause. As a particular case of this one can show that a set of clauses implies another set. Suppose that we wish to show that Δ logically implies the formula ψ. Then it is sufficient to show that $\Delta \cup \{\sim \psi\}$ is unsatisfiable.

We state without proof the results on soundness and completeness of resolution.

Theorem 3.2.6 Soundness *If there is a resolution deduction of a clause Φ form a database of clauses Δ, then Δ logically implies Φ.*

Thus resolution is only capable of deducing statements that are logically implied by the hypotheses.

Theorem 3.2.7 Completeness *If a set of clauses Δ is unsatisfiable, then there is a resolution deduction of the empty cluase from Δ.*

None of the foregoing tells us how to do the resolution. In particular it does not tell us how to choose which pair of literals to use at a
given stage of the resolution process. There are several strategies that
have been described. The interested reader is referred to the book by
Genesereth and Nilsson [39] for a survey and further references. One
special case will be of interest to us later so we describe it here.

In *directed resolution* the clause to be proved consists only of positive literals $\{\phi_1, \ldots, \phi_n\}$ and the database consists of *directed clauses*
that is clauses containing only one positive literal which is either at
the beginning or the end. (Clauses containing only one positive literal
are called Horn clauses.) We can then attempt to resolve the clauses
following the order in which they appear in the clause to be proved.
Clauses in the database where the positive literal is at the begining
give backward resolution in which negative clauses are derived from
other negative clauses. If the positive literal is at the end of the clause
we have forward resolution in which positive clauses are derived from
positive clauses.

3.3   A Categorical Model

Before turning to other examples of reasoning methods I want to pick
up on an idea that I touched on earlier when I talked about proofs
as programs. Category theoretic methods have been used in logic for
some time. The idea of a topos is specifically devised to model logic
in a category theoretic way. I do not propose to go into that here.
The interested reader can consult [62].

My interest at this point is to show how a categorical framework
provides a way of integrating some of the ideas from the section on
search and logical reasoning, without choosing one or the other as the
representation.

Recall that a category $\mathcal{C}$ consists of a collection of objects $Obj(\mathcal{C})$
and for every pair A, B of elements of $Obj(\mathcal{C})$ a set $Mor(A, B)$ (or
$\mathcal{C}(A, B)$ if i is desired to make the category explicit.) There is a notion
of composition of morphisms

$$Mor(A, B) \times Mor(B, C) \rightarrow Mor(A, C)$$

which is required to be associative. Further for every object A in $Obj(C)$ there is a morphism Id_A which acts as both a left and right identity for composition of morphisms. Every category C has associated to it a category C^{op} with the same objects and with the senses of the morphisms reversed so that $C^{op}(A, B) = C(B, A)$.

The maps between categories are called functors. Given two categories C and D a (covariant) *functor* T maps $T : Obj(C) \to Obj(D)$ and morphism sets $T : C(A, B) \to D(T(A), T(B)$ so that composition is respected that is we have $T(f \circ g) = T(f) \circ T(g)$. A functor $S : C^{op} \to D$ is called a contravariant functor $S : C \to D$. Evidently in this case the composition of morphisms becomes $T(f \circ g) = T(g) \circ T(f)$.

As an example category that is particularly relevant to our context we can take the category $\mathcal{L}$ whose objects are logical formulae and whose morphisms $\mathcal{L}(p, q)$ are "proofs" of formula q under the "assumptions" p.

The algebraic approach to problems depends on an ability to build complex problems from simpler ones. Hence the importance of notions of composition and decomposition of objects. Category theory is particularly suited to this. We review some of the ideas here. The simplest notions are products and co-products. We introduce these through their universal properties. (this is a simplified version of what in category theory is called a limit, readers wishing to see an exposition based upon this language should refer to [81].)

Let C be a catgory and let A and B be objects of C, then the *product* $A \times B$ in C is an object with projection maps $\pi_A : A \times B \to A$ and $\pi_B : A \times B \to B$ such that given any pair of morphisms $f \epsilon Mor(X, A)$ and $g \epsilon Mor(X, B)$ there is a unique map $(f, g) \epsilon Mor(X, A \times B)$ such that $\pi_A \circ (f, g) = f$ and $\pi_B \circ (f, g) = g$. The *coproduct* $A \coprod B$ is defined in a dual manner. That is there are inclusion morphisms $i_A : A \to A \coprod B$ and $i_B : B \to A \coprod B$ such that given any object X and a pair of morphisms $f : A \to X$ and $g :\to X$ there is a unique morphism $(f \coprod g) : A \coprod B \to X$ such that $(f \coprod g) \circ i_A = f$ and $(f \coprod g) \circ i_B = g$.

In the logic example above the product is the $\wedge$ of two formulae and the universal property says that a proof of a conjunction is given by a proof of each of the conjuncts. The coproduct is a disjunction.

Before proceeding to a more detailed description of how category theory applies to the reasoning models that we have outline we need to introduce two more notions. Those of pushout and pullback which generalise coproduct and product respectively.

Definition 3.3.1 *Let* $f \epsilon$ *Mor*(C, A) *and* $g \epsilon$ *Mor*(C, B) *the pushout of* f *and* g *is a commutative diagram*

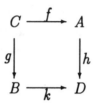

having the following universal property. Given any set of morphisms $m_C \ \epsilon \ Mor(C, X)$, $m_A \ \epsilon \ Mor(A, X)$ *and* $m_B \ \epsilon \ Mor(B, X)$ *such that*

$$m_A \circ f = m_B \circ g = m_C$$

there is a unique morphism $m_D \ \epsilon \ Mor(D, X)$ *such that* $h \circ m_D = m_A$ *and* $k \circ m_D = m_B$.

Dually the pull back is defined as follows. Suppose that we have morphisms $h \ \epsilon \ Mor(A, D)$ *and* $k \epsilon \ Mor(B, D)$ *then the* pullback *is given by a commutative diagram*

$$
\begin{array}{ccc}
C & \xrightarrow{\ f\ } & A \\
{\scriptstyle g}\downarrow & & \downarrow{\scriptstyle h} \\
B & \xrightarrow[\ k\ ]{} & D
\end{array}
$$

having the following universal property. Given any set of morphisms $p_A \epsilon \ Mor(X, A)$, $p_B \epsilon \ Mor(X, B)$ *and* $p_C \epsilon \ Mor(X, D)$ *such that* $k \circ p_D = p_B$ *and* $h \circ p_D = p_A$ *there is a unique morphism* $p_C \epsilon \ Mor(X, C)$ *such that* $f \circ p_C = p_A$ *and* $g \circ p_C = p_B$.

The pushout corresponds to ∨ where the two components are not disjoint, but share a common component disjunct (the object C.) The pullback corresponds to the case of a conjunction where the components share a common conjunct (the object D).

An interesting example of a pullback arises in the case of substitution. A predicate p with variable set X can be thought of as a morphism $p \rightarrow X$. The "substitution " is then a morphism $A \rightarrow X$ and the pull back of p along $A \rightarrow X$ is the substitution. Unification from this point of view is a question of finding a common pullback.

The main point of this section however has to be that all these notions make sense for graphs, so that the category theory viewpoint provides some measure of unity between the approaches. Let us now address that issue.

The aspect of the graph approach to search that I am particularly concerned to capture is the notion of decomposition. I will begin with a definition for the category of graphs. It is only necessary to give the morphisms. Given two graphs $\mathcal{G}_i = (N_i, E_i), i = 1, 2$ the graph is itself a category, whose objects are the nodes and whose morphisms are the edges (directed as necessary) with the addition of identity morphisms for each node. A morphism between two graphs is simply a covariant functor between the corresponding categories. The result of a sucessful search in a graph is a path in the the graph. This is a special graph having at most one morphism between any pair of nodes. In categorical terms then search decomposition reduces to the solution of the following problem. Given the graph morphism $P \rightarrow Q$, representing a map of the problem P onto another problem Q, and a solution $G \rightarrow Q$ find the pull back S and a solution in S that makes the following diagram commute.

The morphism $P \rightarrow Q$ can be thought of as mapping the problem on P into a "simpler" problem Q for which a solution $G \to Q$ already exists. One tries to pull this back to a solution to the original problem.

3.4   Default Reasoning.

In the course of everyday life we will often make use of implicit assumptions that are not in fact universally valid. We will conclude for example that a given bird flies; that an elephant is grey, or that a Quaker is a pacifist. These are examples of default reasoning. Its value in reducing the efficiency of human reasoning capabilities lies in the fact that most of the time these conclusions are true. Nevertheless the conclusions are not in fact universally true. Therefore if we intend to try and capture this kind of reasoning capability in an intelligent system we must formalise the process.

I will describe two approaches to default reasoning. In the first *default theories* the model is formal logic. The second approach is relevant when the knowledge is structured in a network form.

3.4.1   Default Theories

Default theories are akin to modal logic in that they add to conventional first order logic features designed to capture the information necessary for default reasoning. The work of Ray Reiter [84] has been central in this area.

Default theories are based upon the notion of a *default rule*. These take the form

$$\frac{A(x) : C(x)}{B(x)}$$

each of $A(x), C(x)$, and $B(x)$ is a well formed formula. $A(x)$ represents the hypotheses, $C(x)$ a consistency check and $B(x)$ the conclusion to be drawn in case the consistency check is verified. For example we might have the following default rule.

$$\frac{Bird(x) : Flies(x)}{Flies(x)}$$

The intuitive interpretation of this is "If x is a bird and it is consistent that x flies then x flies". Thus we can draw the conclusion that x

flies in the absence of any reason to believe that x cannot fly. For example knowledge that x is a kiwi would make flies(x) inconsistent with the data we already know.

We can model the process of reasoning in a default theory as follows. There is a database Δ of conventional wffs. In addition there is a collection $\mathcal{D}$ of default rules. These can be used to form an extension $\mathcal{E}(\Delta, \mathcal{D})$ of Δ. Each of these possible extensions forms a consistent world extending Δ. However as we shall see in a moment there can be several extensions of the same system and these need not be mutually consistent. We will use a more compact notation $A(x) : C(x)/B(x)$ rather than the displayed form that we used above in our examples.

Suppose that our system contains the following default rules.

1. $Quaker(x) : Pacifist(x)/Pacifist(x)$

2. $Republican(x) :\sim Pacifist(x)/ \sim Pacifist(x)$

Then the database $Quaker(Richard), Republican(Richard)$ has two mutually inconsistent extensions:
$Quaker(Richard), Republican(Richard), Pacifist(Richard)$ and
$Quaker(Richard), Republican(Richard), \sim Pacifist(Richard)$.

Since both are consistent we may choose either one to extend our beliefs about the world but we cannot choose both. This implies that if we subsequently discover new information that impugns one of the default assumptions we will then have to redo our reasoning. This ambiguity of extension is a topic to which we shall return shortly.

One interesting aspect of this method is that it allows us to represent the *Closed World Assumption.* In a closed world we assume that we have all the evidence that we need to reach positive conclusions. Thus a closed world assumption about some predicate $P(x)$ can be represented as a default rule.

$$\frac{:\sim P(x)}{\sim P(x)}$$

So that if it is consistent to believe that $P(x)$ is not true then we can conclude that $P(x)$ is false. Or put another way in the absence of evidence for $P(x)$ we can conclude that $P(x)$ is false.

Before we conclude the discussion of default theories we should note that they fit nicely into the reasoning paradigm of inference that we discussed earlier in section 3.2.1. In particular it is clear how one would modify an inference system to use default rules. What is new is that the choice of the default to pursue can lead to quite different worlds.

3.4.2   Default Reasoning in Networks

The frame mechanism as we saw earlier also has built into it a default capability which allows subclasses to inherit the properties from their parent class. Thus a class bird would have a slot indicating that birds fly. 'Tweety' being a bird should fly however as a member of the class kiwi 'Tweety' will inherit from kiwi an explicit override of any flight capability.

This suggests another mechanism for default reasoning that would be appropriate for network representations, particularly those representations that use **IS-A** links. An early reference to this approach is the work of Etherington and Reiter [37]. More recent work has been done by Lokendra Shastri [90]. Since both methods use the reasoning paradigm attached to the representation as a basis for the default reasoning it is particularly appropriate for us to review their work here.

The approach of Etherington and Reiter is to introduce into the network additional link types that carry different degrees of inheritance. This seems to be a natural extension of the idea of an **IS-A** link. Specifically there are five link types.

1. A *strict IS-A* B, meaning all A's are B's.

2. A *strict ISN'T-A* B, meaning A's are never B's

3. A *default IS-A* B, usually A's are B's

4. A *default ISN'T-A* B, usually A's are not B's

5. A *exception* link B, A is an exception to this link type.

The exception link is used to cancel the effect of a specific link. If one thinks of the links as providing specific steps in a reasoning chain then an exception link provides a way of defeating a particular chain of reasoning for a specific class or instance. Such a link will always parallel another link of one of the other types.

Natural though this system is it still leaves the ambiguity of the Republican Quaker that we had in the default rules system since the *default IS-A* links will still permit the drawing of the two mutually contradictory conclusions. Besides the inherent problems associated with the ambiguous conclusions this raises additional problems for parallelizing the inferencing in a network since both conclusions will be drawn. (To be fair a parallel implementation of a default rules system will have the same problem.) Since one of the advantages of networks is that they lend themselves to parallelism it would be desirable to resolve this difficulty. Shastri's model which we describe next gives one approach.

3.4.3 Default and Ambiguity

In the previous section we saw that default reasoning can lead to ambiguity in the sense that we are able to extend a set of facts to two different sets of conclusions that contain contradictory conclusions. In the absence of additional assumptions it is unreasonable to expect to be able to resolve this difficulty. One approach to a resolution has been given by Lokendra Shastri [90]. The approach mixes a number of ideas that have been touched upon earlier and I will describe it here.

Spreading Activation

One of the earliest ideas for reasoning in a semantic network is that of *spreading activation*. Suppose that we have a network that represents knowledge about some domain. Amongst the problems that we can pose are recognition and inheritance. In the recognition problem we are given a number of properties of some object from the domain and asked to determine the object. The inheritance problem is a partial converse to the recognition problem, given an object we must infer the value of one of its attributes. Thus a recognition system should identify "Richard" given the properties of Republican and Quaker. Conversely given a ripe apple the system is likely to infer that the apple is red, even though the system may know about Granny Smiths or Cox's Orange Pippins.

The spreading activation solution to the recognition problem can be described as follows. Imagine that the knowledge is represented in a network. (The simple example of Richard is depicted in the figure).

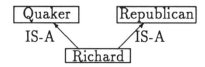

Then as each concept is recognised — Quaker and Republican in the diagram above — the links leading from the concept pass the activation of the concept to the neighboring concepts, causing them to fire. IS-A links are activatory. Other kinds of links such as the ISN'T-A links that we described above would be inhibitory links that will prevent firing. When a "sufficient" number (taking into account both inhibitory and activating links) of incoming links at a concept have become active that concept itself is also activated, which in turn causes it to activate its outgoing links and spreading the activation through the network.

Spreading activation has a psychological appeal because through the idea of priming it explains results like the "Mac-hine" trick with which we introduced networks. In a more sophisticated guise it is the basis of neural networks, with the important distinction that in a neural network the concepts can be stored as patterns of activity rather than as single nodes. Our interest in this mechanism at the moment is in its potential for handling ambiguity and multiple inheritance.

Shastri's Knowledge Representation

In Shastri's system an agent has a priori knowledge about the world that contains distributional information about the values of the attributes. Thus to encompass the fact that apples can be red or green it will have a distribution for the colour of apples that might take the form {(RED 60), (GREEN 40)}. This will justify the inference that an apple is red. Shastri formalises this as follows.

The agent's a priori knowledge consists of the septuple

$$\Theta = (C, \Phi, \lambda, \Lambda, \#, \delta, \ll)$$

where

C is the set of concepts,

Φ is the set of properties,

λ is a mapping from C to the power set of Φ giving the properties attached to a given concept.

\# is a mapping from C to the integers I. If C is a token then $\#C = 1$ whereas if C is a type then $\#C$ is the number of instances of the type that the agent has observed.

δ is the distribution function, which is a mapping $\delta : C \times \Phi \to 2^{C \times I}$,

$\ll$ is a partial order on C, corresponding to the IS-A relation.

It should be noted that the number mapping \# can be extended to

$$\#C[P_1, V_1][P_2, V_2], \ldots, [P_n, V_n] =$$

the number of instances of C observed to have the value V_i for property $P_i, i = 1, \ldots n$.

We can pose the inheritance and recognition problems in this language as follows.

Inheritance
Given:

- $\Theta = (C, \Phi, \lambda, \Lambda, \#, \delta, \ll)$

- $C \epsilon C, P \epsilon \lambda(C)$, and

- an enumeration of possible answers, that is a subset of $\Lambda(P)$

$$V - SET = (V_1, V_2, \ldots, V_n),$$

Find: $V^*\epsilon V - SET$ such that among members of $V - SET$, V^* is the most likely value of property P for concept C. In other words, find $V^*\epsilon V - SET$ such that for any $V_i\epsilon V - SET$, the best estimate of $\#C[P, V^*] \geq$ the best estimate of $\#C[P, V_i]$ for all other $V_i\epsilon V - SET$.

Recognition

Given:

- $\Theta = (\mathbf{C}, \Phi, \lambda, \Lambda, \#, \delta, \ll)$,

- an enumeration of possible answers, that is a set of concepts $C - SET = C_1, \ldots C_n$,

- a description, $DESCR$, consisting of a sets of property value pairs $- [P_1, V_1], \ldots [P_m, V_m]$ such that:

$$\forall [P_j, V_j]\epsilon DESCR,$$

$$V_j\epsilon\Lambda(P_j) \text{ and } P_j\epsilon \cap_{C\epsilon C-SET} \lambda(C)$$

In other words, each property mentioned in the description should apply to every concept on the $C - SET$, and the values specified for these properties should be appropriate.

Find: $C^*\epsilon C - SET$ such that *relative* to the concepts specified in $C - SET$, C^* is the most likely concept described by $DESCR$.

The most interesting application of this formalism it to combining evidence. Let us consider the following problem, borrowed from Shastri [90] page 60.

C = APPLE, GRAPE, RED, GREEN, SWEET, SOUR

Φ = has-taste, has-colour

$\lambda(APPLE), \lambda(GRAPE)$ = has-taste, has-colour

$\lambda(RED) = \lambda(GREEN) = \lambda(SWEET) = \lambda(SOUR) = \emptyset$

$\Lambda(has-colour) = RED, GREEN; \Lambda(has-taste) = SWEET, SOUR$

$\#(APPLE) = 100$

$$\delta(APPLE, has - color) = (RED\ 60), (GREEN\ 40)$$

$$\delta(APPLE, has - taste) = (SWEET\ 70), (SOUR\ 30)$$

$\#(GRAPE) = 50$

$$\delta(GRAPE, has - colour) = (RED\ 5), (GREEN\ 45)$$

$$\delta(GRAPE, has - taste) = (SWEET\ 30), (SOUR\ 20)$$

#RED = 65, #GREEN = 85; #SWEET = 100, #SOUR = 50; $\ll$ is given by: $\emptyset$.

Given this information a rational agent is likely to conclude that a RED object is probably an APPLE and that a SWEET object is also an APPLE. Since in each case the preponderance of objects with these properties are apples. But if it knows that the object is both RED and SWEET it is less clear what conclusion should be drawn. The difficulty is that although we know the distribution of the colour of the apples and the distribution of the taste we do not know the values for the combinations $#APPLE(has - taste, SWEET)(has - colour, RED)$. We can formalize this as follows. We suppose that we have a concept A represented by a matrix with rows R and columns C and entries a_{ij}, where

$$R_i = #A[P_1, v_i P_1]$$

$$C_j = #A[P_2, v_j P_2]$$

$$N = #A = \Sigma R_i = \Sigma C_j$$

$$a_{ij} = #A[P_1, v_i P_1][P_2, v_j P_2]$$

We have used $v_i P$ to denote the ith possible value of the property P. The $R's$ represent row sums and the $C's$ column sums.

The a_{ij}'s are unknown and are to be determined on the basis of N, R_i, C_j. A **macro-configuration** is a specifiaction of all the a_{ij}'s. A **micro-configuration** is a complete specification of a distribution given not only the number of objects having each pair of property values but also their identities. A micro-configuration is called *feasible* if it satisfies the constraints imposed by the row and column sums. The *most probable macro-configuration* is that supported by the greatest number of feasible micro-configurations.

If ω denotes the number of micro-configurations supporting a macro-configuration, then we have

$$\omega = \frac{N!}{\prod_{i=1}^{n} \prod_{j=1}^{m} a_{ij}!}$$

This must be maximised subject to the constraints

$$\forall i \sum_{j=1}^{m} a_{ij} = R_i;$$

$$\forall j \sum_{i=1}^{n} a_{ij} = C_j;$$

$$\sum_{i=1}^{n} \sum_{j=1}^{m} a_{ij} = N$$

Using Lagrange multipliers one obtains the maximum likelyhood estimate

$$a_{ij} = \frac{R_i C_j}{N}$$

Let us see how this applies to the case of inheritance. We recall the inheritance problem

Given:

- $\Theta = (\mathbf{C}, \Phi, \lambda, \Lambda, \#, \delta, \ll)$

- $C \epsilon C, P \epsilon \lambda(C)$, and

- an enumeration of possible answers, that is a subset of $\Lambda(P)$

$$V - SET = (V_1, V_2, \ldots, V_n),$$

Find: $V^* \epsilon V - SET$ such that among members of $V - SET$, V^* is the most likely value of property P for concept C. In other words, find $V^* \epsilon V - SET$ such that for any $V_i \epsilon V - SET$, the best estimate of $\#C[P, V^*] \geq$ the best estimate of $\#C[P, V_i]$ for all other $V_i \epsilon V - SET$.

Suppose that we are given two concepts C and B, and a property P such that

1. $C \ll B$,

2. $\delta(C, P)$ is not known, but

3. $\delta(B, P)$ is known,

then in the absence of any other information the best estimate of

$$\#C[P,V] = \#B[P,V] \times \frac{\#C}{\#B}.$$

This leads to the following rule on the well-formedness of the conceptual structure.

> The agent stores all distributions that are important to him and that cannot be estimated accurately on the basis of information available at concepts higher up in the conceptual structure.

As long as there is only one place from which the agent might inherit the estimate this principle is fine. However as we have seen in the case of the Republican Quaker there can be two relevant concepts from which inheritance is possible.

We conclude our review of Shastri's work with his discussion of multiple inheritance. We will confine ourselves to the simple case of multiple inheritance from concepts with a single parent.

Suppose that we have the following information.

$\delta(\text{QUAKER, has-belief}) = (\text{PACIFIST 7})(\text{NON-PACIFIST 3})$

$\delta(\text{REPUBLICAN, has-belief}) = (\text{PACIFIST 16})(\text{NON-PACIFIST 64})$

$\delta(\text{PERSON, has-belief}) = (\text{PACIFIST 38})(\text{NON-PACIFIST 96})$

If we use these figures and the formula

$$\frac{\#Quaker[has-belief, Pacifist] \times \#Republican[has-belief, Pacifist]}{\#Person[has-belief, Pacifist]}$$

as best estimate of the overlap #Republican-Quaker[has-belief, Pacifist]. We get the value $(7 \times 16)/38$. A similar argument gives the value $3 \times 64)96$ for the estimate of #Republican-Quaker[has-belief, Non-pacifist]. Thus a rational agent would be about 1.5 times as likely to believe that Richard is a pacifist than that he is a non-pacifist.

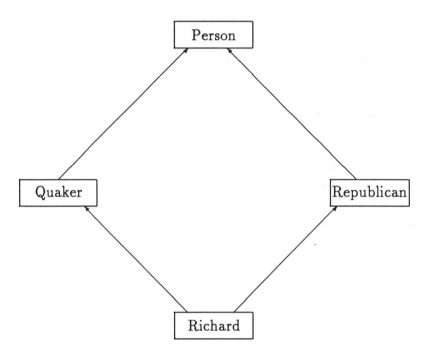

Figure 3.1: The Republican Quaker Triangle

In general we will have concepts $B_1 \ldots B_n$ relevant to C with respect to property P and Ω a common parent for all the B_k. then the best estimate is given by

$$\frac{\#C[P,V_j]}{\#C[P,V_q]} = \left[\frac{\#\Omega[P,V_q]}{\#\Omega[P,V_j]}\right]^{n-1} \times \prod_{k=1}^{n}\left[\frac{\#B_k[P,V_j]}{\#B_k[P,V_q]}\right]$$

provided that $\delta(\Omega, P)$ is known. The interested reader can refer to Shastri for more details. Similar considerations apply to the recognition problem. Futhermore the more complex multiple inheritance problems suggest principles for structuring the concept tree so as to allow for the kind of disambiguation that we have described for the simple case.

3.5 Procedural Reasoning

In procedural reasoning the knowledge is stored in terms of an explicit algorithm for determining the value of the item sought. It is thus in some sense antithetical to the currently accepted paradigm for Artificial Intelligence, which places considerable emphasis on the separation of knowledge from procedure. However there are places where procedural knowledge plays a legitimate role.

One case that arises quite naturally in systems that use frame based representation is the use of slot values that contain procedures for determining the value of a specific attribute. Thus a process control system is likely to refer to the value of a sensor to obtain readings that it needs for monitoring the state of the process.

Another case would be that of a robot that is capable of performing a number of tasks. For tasks that are routine and predictable it makes sense to provide a "canned" procedure that carries out the task, whereas less frequently occurring tasks may be handled by a planning system that constructs a solution when the task is presented. This is in fact closely related to much human learning. In the psychological literature this technique is sometimes called chunking. It forms the basis for the learning component of the SOAR system [61]; Korf's macro operators [57] are also examples of this technique. In view of its importance for constructing intelligent systems I will describe a model of it here.

Another place where proceduural knowledge is important in Artificial Intelligence is in the construction of the systems themselves. Even though a system may appear to use a declarative paradigm the computational engine itself cannot do this. Any practical system must make use of some set of rules for coping with indeterminacy. Indeed the very definition of an algorithm requires determinacy at each step. So that even if the knowledge is declarative its use must be reduced to a procedural implementation. Central to this reduction are questions of efficiency and tractability. It will be necessary to discuss these issues.

3.5.1 Chunking

A system that learns must have some way of storing the knowledge that it acquires and of determining what information it should store. The ability to do this requires that the system be able to specify subtasks and their solutions. The details of how this is done will depend on the domain in which the system works. However there are sufficient similarities underlying the basic idea that one can give a generic description.

For the purpose at hand we define a *task* T to be a specification consisting of a triple (s_0, G, Ω) where

- s_0 is the specification of an initial state,

- G is the specification of the goal state,

- Ω is a set of "operators" that the system has for effecting the task.

We further assume that there is some rule $\otimes$ for composition of tasks. A solution for a task is a sequence of operators that transforms the initial state into the final state. More formally a task will be called elementary if it has a solution consisting of the application of a single operator. A solution to a general task T is the expression of T as the composition $T_1 \otimes T_2 \otimes \ldots T_n$ where each T_i is an elementary task. An explicit composition of elementary tasks is a *chunk*. (A chunk as defined here is similar to one of Korf's macro operators.)

One more concept is needed in order to be able to make sensible use of chunking and that is a notion of task mapping. This notion must satisfiy a property that allows it to be used in conjunction with task decomposition. To wit — it must be the case that if two tasks are equivalent then a decomposition of one must produce a decomposition of the other. A natural way of describing this is to use the language of category theory. We introduce the notion of a **chunking** category.

For a chunking category we must have

- A collection of tasks T,

- A notion of task maps so that for any pair T_1, T_2 of tasks there is a (possibly empty) set of task maps $Map(T_1, T_2)$.

- There are composition rules $\otimes_1, \ldots \otimes_k$ for tasks which respect the isomorphism notion attached to the mappings of problems.

In such a category tasks that are expressed as the composition of elementary tasks can be regarded as being 'new' elementary tasks and added to to the list of elementary tasks. We can quickly illustrate the idea with two examples.

The first example is the LOGIC-THEORIST of Newell and Simon [74] as described by O'Rorke in [78]. This is a program that proves theorems drawn from Russell and Whitehead's "Principia Mathematica". A task consists of a theorem to be proved. Initially what is known is the axioms and the operation which combines axioms and known theorems to produce new theorems. Specifically composition of tasks is given by chaining together elementary tasks obtained from the two basic schemata.

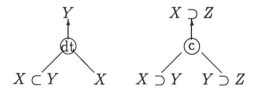

The left schema corresponds to detachment (dt) and the right one to chaining (c). Schema are the elementary tasks. Composition of tasks is obtained by joining the concluding arrow of one task to the right child of the lowest schema in the other task. Maps within the category are given by unification.

The second example is Korf's solution of the Rubik's cube puzzle [57]. Here composition is exactly following one sequence of moves with another sequence of moves. Korf's condition of serial decomposability is precisely what is required to be able to use his search method to find a task decomposition that solves the problem. We review the ideas here, the interested reader is referred to Korf [57].

Korf uses a "state vector" representation of a problem. A point in the state space is accordingly represented by the values $(s_1, \ldots s_n)$ of a set of vectors. Thus to represent the states in Rubik's cube the variables are the cubies and their values encode both their position and orientation. In the language of features there is a feature for each cubie, and the values of each feature correspond to the location and orientation of the cubie. Features and state vectors are dual concepts (much as coordinate values and coordinate functions are); there is no difference in their informational content. A state vector is given by evaluating a set of features, the features are recoverable by taking specific coordinates of the state vector.

For a macro problem solver a solution to a problem comes in the form of a macro table. A macro is simply a move sequence that serves to transform the value of one component of the solution vector into the goal value. In order to be able to find macros which will solve the problem it is necessary to be able to order the state variables in such a way that the macros reduce each value in order without destroying what has already been achieved. In more formal terms we can describe Korf's results in terms of his notion of *serial decomposability* as follows.

Definition 3.5.1 *A* solution order *is a ordering of the state variables* $(s_1, \ldots, s_n)$ *of a state vector.*

A solution order is thus a selection of the order in which the components of the state vector are to be brought to the goal values.

Definition 3.5.2 *A* function f *is* serially decomposable *with respect to a particular solution order iff there exists a set of vector functions*

f_i for $1 \le i \le n$, where each f_j is a function from V^j to V, and V^j is the set of i-ary vectors with components chosen from V, which satisfy the following condition:

$$\forall s \epsilon S, f(s) = f(s_1, \ldots, s_n) = (f_1(s_1), f_2(s_1, s_2), \ldots, f_n(s_1, \ldots, s_n))$$

A macro is serially decomposable with respect to a solution order if each of the operators in it are.

Definition 3.5.3 *A problem is* serially decomposable *if there exists a solution order such that every move is serially decomposable with respect to it.*

In a serially decomposable problem there is some way of ordering the features of the problem so that the effect of a move on a feature depends only on the values of those features that precede it in the solution order. The significance of serial decomposability is in the following theorem.

Theorem 3.5.4 *If a problem is serially decomposable, then there is a macro table for it.*

This theorem provides a satisfying conclusion to Korf's work because it seems clear that it delimits effectively the domain of problems to which Korf's method applies. Each macro solves a particular task and the serial decomposability guarantees that the problem can be decomposed into a sequence of subtasks.

3.5.2 Algorithms and Implementation

In a sense this brief section is an advance notice of what is to come in the sequel. I remarked earlier that when one turns to the actual problem of implementing an AI system then one is entering a procedural world in that the computer is an algorithmic device, (it is perhaps arguable that a neural net is not one, nevertheless implementation of them are.) For the moment it will be enough to point out the places in which this procedurality become apparent.

The two basic reasoning methods that we have described are search and logical reasoning. Both of these were presented in a nondeterministic way. That is to say there were choice points in the description of the process that is to be gone through in the reasoning. Any implementation should disambiguate these choices. Ideally one uses the knowledge available to one to make this choice. Usually this involves some assessment of which choice is likely to be best. The rules that guide this assessment can be either declarative or procedural. In any case what one has at the end is a reduction of what may have been a declarative solution to a procedural one. In the next section we will look at some of the ways in which one might reduce the scope of the choices that occur in both the logical and search reasoning cases.

3.6   Heuristics

As we have seen, one of the characteristics of problems in Artificial Intelligence is the prevalence of large search spaces. Heuristics provide a way of reducing the amount of search that may be required. The topic has been the subject of considerable effort in the AI community. Important early work was done by Newell and Simon [74] in their creation of general problem solver (GPS). The work of Banerji and Ernst [8] and Ernst and Goldstein [35] developed GPS into a formal system. Korf's work [57] is a sophisticated development along the GPS lines. In another direction the work of Pearl in his book [79] considers the case of best first search algorithms in general, with emphasis on quantitative results. A third line of development is that exemplified by large systems such as SOAR, (which I will consider at length in chapter 6) and Lauriere's ALICE [63].

I have written at length elsewhere giving an algebraic formulation of heuristic theory [51]. For this reason I have chosen a different approach to reviewing heuristics in AI. This uses a somewhat cruder classification than my earlier one, without entirely abandoning the formal algebraic view. I divide heuristics into two classes, those based upon problem decomposition and those based upon the best first approach. This decomposition is not completely exhaustive but is adequate for the present purposes.

3.6.1 Decomposition Heuristics

GPS is the original decomposition heuristic. By concentrating on fulfilling subgoals of the goal the domain of the search can be sometimes restricted. Rather than giving a full review of GPS I will give a simple model of decomposition that serves as a framework for discussing decomposition heuristics. I will adopt the following semi-formal definition of a problem.

Definition 3.6.1 *A problem is a triple* (I, M, G). *Where* I *is a set of predicates which define the initial state of the problem,* M *is a set of operators that modify the state of the problem and* G *is a set of predicates which define the goal set of the problem.*

It should be remarked that the choice of logical language here is not an essential part of the definition. One could as well define the initial state and the goal in terms of a set of function values.

A solution to the problem consists in finding a sequence of operators from M that when applied in the initial state I will have the effect of making the predicates describing the goal state G true. Suppose that the goal state G can be written as a conjunction $G = A \wedge B$ then we can decompose the problem into a pair of problems (I, M, A) and $(A, M, A \wedge B)$. If we can solve each of these problems then we can solve the original problem. The advantage come if we can show that each of the component problems (I, M, A) and $(A, M, A \wedge B)$ are simpler.

Fool's Disk serves as an instructive example of this technique. In this problem (originally solved by Ernst and Goldstein [35]), four concentric rings are each divided into eight sectors containing an integer. The rings are free to rotate about their common center. The problem is to rotate the discs so that the sum along each radius is 12.

If we make the obvious reduction that the innermost disc need not be moved at all then we have a search space with 8^3 states. Following Ernst and Goldstein we can introduce the intermediate problems

1. Move the rings so that the sum on each pair of orthogonal diameters is 48.

2. Stating from a position satisfying the final condition of 1 move the discs to a position in which the sum along each diameter is 24.

3. Starting from a position satisfying the final condition of 2 solve the original problem.

Now what makes this method work is that the move sets for each problem can be substantially reduced. In fact we have the following move sets:

1. Move any set of rings through 45 degrees,

2. Move any set of rings through 90 degrees,

3. Move any set of rings through 180 degrees.

Thus each intermediate problem has just 8 moves and we have achieved a reduction of the search space to 8×3.

Three points need to be made about the above example. First is that much of the significance of Ernst and Goldsteins paper lies in the fact that their system discovered this decomposition. Second, there is an implicit assumption in the calculation of the search reduction that the intermediate problems lie on some solution path, should they fail to do so then backtracking will be necessary with a concomitant loss of the advantage supposedly to be gained from the decomposition. Finally we note that as we proceed towards the solution we are able to preserve the gains of the previous steps.

Much of the succeeding work in the area of problem decomposition has addressed itself to the the last of these problems. It is one to which we will return in chapter 6 when we discuss the structuring of large scale systems.

Notable in the way in which we have described this approach is the use of predicates to describe the goal and the assumption that we can write the goal as a conjunction of subgoals. In fact this is, as I remarked earlier, not specifically a consequence of the logical representation. The purely algebraic formalisation of [77], [10] and [51] allows one to obtain the same kind of decomposition independently of the logical language. As witness to this I will now give a dual formulation that has this more algebraic flavour.

Definition 3.6.2 *A free problem P consists of a triple (S, Ω, a) where*

- S *is a set called the state space of the problem*

- Ω *is a set called the move set of the problem,*

- *a is a partial map*

$$a : S \times \Omega \rightarrow S$$

  which represents the action of the move set on the state space.

Composition of moves correspond to composition of the associated partial maps. We thus obtain a semi-group structure for the action of Ω on S. We would like to do something analogous to the notion of a quotient structure. Specifically we want to cover the state space S by a collection $(S_1, \ldots S_k)$ of subsets and view the problem as one of navigating between the initial subset and a subset containing the goal. This decomposes the problem into one of first constructing a chain of subsets between the start and the goal and then one of moving within each subset.

The viability of the method depends upon finding reasonable candidates for the subset decompositions. Two methods suggest themselves.

1. Let Ω^* denote the set of all possible move sequences. Choose a subset Λ of Ω^* which is closed under composition. Then express S as a union of sets $S(x) = \{\lambda(x) \mid \lambda \in \Lambda\}$

2. Choose some subset T of S and let Ω_T be the subset of Ω^* consisting of all move sequences leaving T set wise invariant. Then express S as a union of Ω_T invariant sets.

The first of these methods is used by Banerji in his solution of sliding tile puzzles [9]. the second is the basis of the fool's disk solution given earlier.

3.6.2 Best First Searches

We have seen that many of the reasoning procedures can be viewed as searches. At each step there is a choice that must be made as to which of the rules is to be applied and in the case where the rule applies in more than one way which application is to be preferred. Best first searches use some estimate of the amount of progress that a particular choice will make to decide between the various alternatives. As an example of this we consider the case of reasoning in a production system.

Recall that a production system represents its knowledge as a set of rules in the form **IF** *condition* **THEN** *action*. Suppose that we have elected to use a forward chaining method, then the reasoning loop takes the following form.

1. Traverse the knowledge base and note all the rules that fire.

2. Select one of the rules that has fired and perform its action clause.

The second item is the one that calls for a choice. The rule that is used to make this choice is based upon a heuristic. Options are

- If the rules are ordered, act on the first one;

- If the rules have a priority, act on the one with the highest priority;

- Act on the most specific rule;

- Act on the rule that most nearly matches the goal.

Indeed a substantial production system is likely to have a number of rules whose sole purpose is to determine how to make the choice. Rules of this type are usually referred to as meta-rules. We shall see more detailed examples later when we come to discuss SOAR and ALICE in the construction of large scale systems.

Chapter 4

Language and Reasoning

Thus far I have discussed both knowledge representation and reasoning methods in somewhat abstract terms. It is however the thesis of this work that the way in which one represents knowledge is inherently biased by the language that is used for the discussion. More accurately I should say that there is a strong interaction between language, reasoning and representation. The aim of this chapter is to show how the actual representation chosen for an AI problem not only biases the algorithm but also determines the language used to talk about it.

Of particular interest is the actual languages that can be used in AI. We are concerned with the match between a problem representation and a particular language. The chapter will incorporate a discussion of several languages that can be used in AI. Each language is chosen because it illustrates a specific aspect of the representation or reasoning problem. The descriptions of the languages may be somewhat unusual in that I will not attempt to provide a full introduction to any of them – this is better done in books devoted to the language in question. Rather my approach is akin to that taken in discussions of programming languages, where a given language is used to illustrate a specific issue.

4.1 LISP and Functional Languages

LISP is the most venerable of the AI languages having been created during the years 1956-62 by John McCarthy. There are several books on LISP to which the reader can refer for a detailed description of the language. Readers who want to see LISP treated as an AI language should consult the book of Winston and Horn [101]. For a less AI oriented viewpoint there are the books of Stark [93] and Wilensky [100].

The early years of LISP were characterised by the emergence of a large number of dialects of the language. That this was possible is a tribute to the flexibility and extensibility of the language. In the middle of the 1980's Common LISP emerged as a attempt at standardisation of LISP. As with many such efforts what emerged is a large language that attempts to satisfy all the competing interests. Fortunately I shall not delve deeply enough into LISP to need to take a position on the merits or otherwise of Common LISP.

As is by now well known LISP stands for (LIS)t Processing language. It is the ability to handle lists easily that most characterises lisp. Its other main characteristic is the extensibility secured by the convenient method for defining functions. While this does not of itself make LISP a functional language it allows for the use of a functional programming style. The other dominant influence on Lisp is the fact that it is an interpreted language.

The fundamental data structures of LISP are s-expressions. These are not quite lists. They are the natural objects once one has realised that there are to be atoms and lists and certain operations upon them. In more detail, there are three fundamental functions in LISP

- **car** a selector function defined on lists that returns the first element of a list,

- **cdr** a selector function defined on lists that returns the list that is obtained by removing the first element of the list,

- **cons** a constructor function that satisfies

```
( cons  ( car l) ( cdr  l)) = l
```

for any list l.

The definition of **cons** given above leaves something to be desired in that it is only defined on the product of the ranges of **car** and **cdr**. It is to deal with this that s-expressions are introduced. **cdr** is a list valued function defined upon lists, whereas **car** can have a value that is not a list. These data items, to which **cdr** cannot be applied are called *atoms*. The value of **car** is a list or an atom. The empty list *nil* is an atom. The s-expression can now be defined as

Definition 4.1.1 *An* s-expression *is*

1. *an atom or,*

2. *the result of consing together two s-expressions.*

Note that it is legal to cons together two atoms. This gives rise to an s-expression called a *dotted pair*. In fact one can represent lists using dotted pairs. The only thing that one needs in order to be able to do this is to see how to form a list with just one element x. This is realised by means of the dotted pair $(x.nil)$ where *nil* is the empty list. (Recall that nil is also an atom.

Dotted pairs also are the building blocks for *association lists*, which we have previously referred to under the name attribute lists. These are lists of the form:-

$$((attrib_1 . value_1), (attrib_2 . value_2), \ldots (attrib_k . value_k)).$$

Attribute lists for a symbol are manipulated by the special LISP functions, get, putprop, getprop, and remprop. In this case the attribute list is called a property list.

LISP relies for control on two basic mechanisms the function COND (and its relative IF) and recursion. The form of COND is

```
(cond
        (test1   value1)
        (test2   value2)
        . . . .
        (testk   valuek))
```

The value of this function is that corresponding to the first test that returns a non nil value.

In order to be able to do significant things with recursion we must be able to name lisp functions. This is done using *defun* and *lambda* abstraction. This latter is based upon Church's λ notation. The formalism works this way. We represent a function as

(lambda (argument-list) (body))

The function is evaluated by applying it to a specific set of arguments. For example

(lambda (x y) (sum (times x x) (times y y))

defines a function that will compute $x^2 + y^2$. To get an actual value returned we would have to enter

((lambda (x y) (sum (times x x) (times y y)) 3 4)

which would return 25. Lambda functions are sometimes called anonymous functions. Because such functions have no names *defun* provides a way of naming functions. The syntax is

(defun name argument-list body)

Defun will return the name of the function. It binds the name to the corresponding lambda abstraction. Using defun we can define functions that make use of recursion.

The following is a typical recursive program that returns the length of a list *l*,

```
(defun length (list)
      (cond
         ((equal list nil)  0)
         ( t (add1 ( length (cdr list))))))))
```

LISP's strengths are the ease with which it can be extended and the use of a single unifying data structure – the s-expression. The special functions for manipulating property lists allow one to build frames very simply. (Although common LISP provides a constructor DEFSTRUCT that can also be used for this purpose.) It is worth noting that the ability to use anonymous functions can be exploited in this context. Since a property list can contain a pair of the form (display-function (lambda (args) (body)))

This function can be retrieved with

(getprop symbol 'display-function)

The presence of the *lambda* notation in lisp suggests a relation with Church's λ-calculus. I will not go into this relationship here. The interested reader is referred to the book by Gordon [42], where the relationship is discussed at length and an implementation of the λ- calculus in franz lisp is given. Stark [93] also discusses the relationship. Although there are great similarities between the two the implementation details of lisp produce scope rules that are somewhat different from those of the λ-calculus. The fact that one can build a λ- calculator in lisp has as much to do with lisp's facility with lists as any thing else.

4.1.1 Computation in LISP

The computational paradigm for lisp is the function. The basic data structure is the s-expression. A distinction is often made between "pure" lisp and lisp as it is generally used. Pure lisp is, as the name suggests, that part of lisp that most closely adheres to the functional view. This means that functions have no side effects, thus we cannot use defun nor can we do assignments (functions can still be defined using the labels construction.) This purist view is overly restrictive but it does remind one that there are difficulties inherent in sacrificing referential transparency. The restriction against assignments is particularly expensive when it forces the re-evaluation of a function in circumstances where the value that will be returned is the same as one that was returned previously and guaranteed to be so. Put more simply the inability to store values means that they must be recomputed.

When we come to consider how lisp can be used for the kinds of computations that are involved in the reasoning methods we discussed in the previous chapter we observe the following close matches.

Pattern – Action methods match the *cond* function. Indeed the *cond* function is precisely a condition – action pair. Programs and knowledge representation systems that use pattern – action pairs will fit naturally to lisp, with the proviso that lisp has elected a particular way of seeking the match. The programmer may well have to exercise some ingenuity to obtain the order of consideration that is required.

Frames can, as we remarked earlier be implemented quite easily as property lists. Each slot name just become an attribute.

Networks depending on their type can be implemented quite easily. If the links have names then it is quite natural to use property lists. More general networks can be managed but seem somewhat less natural. One could use the functions such as *rplaca* and *rplacd* that perform surgery on lists. These are however dangerous precisely because the do surgery on lists, whereas *cons* creates new lists which is safer but more expensive in terms of storage.

4.1.2   Functional Languages

Functional languages such as LISP and ML (which we will discuss in the next section) are characterised, at least in their pure form by the principle that the value of an expression in the language should depend only on the value of the subexpressions that it contains. This is the principle of referential transparency referred to earlier. In addition functions must themselves be first-class values. This means that they can be the value of an expression, can be passed as an argument and can appear as part of a data structure.

The significance of this for AI programming should be somewhat evident from our discussion of LISP. Specifically it permits us to do the following.

- Functions can be constructed 'on the fly'.

- Functions can be treated as data for reasoning purposes.

- Data structures can contain custom built functions that manipulate the structure.

Clearly an intelligent system must be able to modify its behaviour, the ability to create new functions allows one to model this. That functions can be treated as data allows the system to reason about its actions, since it can take functions apart. The ability to store functions as part of a data structure allows for a natural way to construct frames as we have already remarked.

4.2 ML and the Theory of Types

LISP is an untyped language. Its functions do no type checking. For example the standard factorial function

```
(defun factorial (n)
(cond
((equal n 0) 1)
(t (times n (factorial (sub1 n)))))))
```

will attempt to evaluate (factorial 0.0) with results that depend on the LISP implementation. ML is a functional language that is strongly typed. This has some advantages in the way in which it allows one to reason about expressions.

Functions in ML are applied by writing them next to their arguments so that $f\ x$ and $f(x)$ are equivalent. Function application associates to the left so that $f\ g\ E$ evaluates as $(f\ g)\ E$ where E is an expression and f and g are functions.

While ML will try and infer types without help from the user they can also be supplied explicitly by using the form

<expression> : <type-expression>

There are type operators list, # an infix operator for creating pairs, + an infix operator for direct sums and − > for functions. So that the type of a function is represented as follows:

square = fn :int -> int

Furthermore users can explicitly define polymorphic functions, such as functions that operate on lists. ML provides built in list manipulation functions

null Test for an empty list ,

hd Return head of list,

tl Return tail of list,

:: The infix version of list construction, as lisp's 'cons'.

The composition rule for ML functions is closer to the λ-calculus than the composition rule of LISP. This makes it more straightforward to translate λ-calculus expressions into ML than LISP. With the added ability to do type checking ML deals with nonsense expressions without trying to evaluate them. This has clear benefits when one does pattern matching. With a rich enough polymorphism it is possible to carry over some of the advantages that the type free LISP programming style permits.

Thus we can describe a list processing algorithm using a listype

datatype listype = nil | cons of listel * listype

The built in list manipulators handle the list structure and one creates special functions for handling the type 'listel'. In a similar way one can work with graphs or trees because the list operations are polymorphic and the operations required for the specific element type at hand can be kept in one place. This is in marked contrast to the way in which a strongly typed language like Pascal requires separate implementation for each type of object to be listed.

ML has been presented because it shows that the advantages of strong typing can be had with the flexibility that one associates with an untyped language. This is characteristic of functional languages where the list constructors provide the necessary leavening of polymorphism. Similar advantages would accrue in cases where the basic constructed type were to be something other than a list, provided that the operations that we performed on them admitted this kind of polymorphism. In actual practice lists have proved to be rich enough for most purposes that both ML and LISP use them.

I will end this section with an example of the way in which ML can be used to support a particular application. The example is taken from work of Gordon, Milner, and Wadsworth on Edinburgh LCF [41], indeed it was to support this application that ML was invented. LCF is a system intended for doing logical proofs. An important aim was to produce an interactive system which would find some middle

ground between the exhaustive search methods of a theorem prover
and the repetitiveness of general proof checkers.

Conceptually the idea is to define a proof type so that the syntax
checker can recognize correct ones. In addition though one needs some
procedure for generating such things. The basic idea for this is that
of a *tactic*. We will go into more detail in a moment. A tactic is like
the task decompositions of section 3.5.1. In goal directed reasoning
a proof is broken up into a sequence of subgoals. Thus Gordon et al.
define the following types

```
goal = form # bool
tactic = goal -> (goal list # validation)
validation = thm list -> thm
```

In addition there is another postulated ML type *event*, which may
achieve goals. There is a binary relation of *achievement* between
events and goals. So that we can replace the definition of the validation type by

```
validation = event list -> event
```

A tactic is *valid* if whenever

$$T(g) = [g_1; \ldots; g_n], v$$

for a goal g, then for events $e_1, \ldots, e_n$ which achieve $g_1, \ldots, g_n$ respectively the event $v[e_1; \ldots; e_n]$ achieves g.

The glue that makes this work is provided by combinators called
tacticals. For example one has

```
ORELSE : tactic # tactic ->  tactic
REPEAT : tactic -> tactic
```

Each of these tacticals has the evident meaning. It is important to
observe that an important part of a tactical is the ability to construct
the corresponding validation.

ML is of interest because it is a language designed to support an
application which has proved to be of serious interest in its own right.
By taking the question of typing seriously it shows that is is possible
to build a computational model in which things like proofs and tactics
are objects that can be manipulated by the system.

4.3   Prolog and Logic Programming

Logic programming represents perhaps the clearest example of the separation of 'what' from 'how', and yet as we shall see this separation is at times more apparent than real. Prolog itself grew out of work by Colmerauer at the University of Marseille-Aix and Kowalski at the University of London. With the appearance of David Warren's Prolog-10 compiler [98] prolog became a real language which demonstrated that logic programming is practical. The de facto standard for prolog was set out in the book of Clocksin and Mellish [24]. This is generally referred to as "Edinburgh Prolog". For an exposition of Prolog in the context of logic programming the book of Ehud Shapiro and Leon Sterling [92] is highly recommended. Neither of these books treat Prolog as primarily an AI language but both contain many examples that are relevant to AI.

4.3.1   Logic Programming

We recall the logic programming model in the form of an abstract interpreter. A logic program consists of facts and clauses. Clauses are written in the form

$$A \leftarrow B_1, B_2, \ldots B_k$$

In addition there is a goal G. The interpreter is to produce either an instance $G\theta$ of G or *failure* if no instance can be found.

Algorithm 4.3.1 A logic Program interpreter
Initialize the resolvent to be the goal G.
While the resolvent is not empty do
  Choose a goal A from the resolvent
  and a clause $A' \leftarrow B_1, \ldots, B_k$ from P
  such that A and A' unify with mguθ
  (exit with failure if no such goal exists).
  Remove A from the resolvent and add $B_1, ldots B_k$.
  Apply θ to the resolvent and to G.
If the resolvent is empty output G, else output failure.

In order to be able to make a practical language out of this abstract interpreter one needs to make the choices involved explicit. The interpreter has to choose which clause to select from the program and which term from the resolvent will be the current subgoal. Given a resolvent $A_1, A_2, \ldots, A_n$, prolog selects the first term A_1. This is *ordered* resolution. In searching for the clause in the program to use for the resolution prolog starts at the top of the program and works down through the list of clauses. This linear strategy results in a depth first traversal of the search tree. Prolog thus exploits the fact that depth first search is efficient in that it does not impose extensive storage overhead in the way that breadth first search does.

As a consequence of these decisions prolog is sensitive to the order in which the clauses occur in the database. This results in minor differences such as the emergence of solutions in different orders and in major one such as completely different program behaviour. An obvious example of this is in recursive programs, where the base case must appear before the recursive ones as in.

```
factorial(0,1).
factorial(N, F) :- N1 is N - 1, factorial(N1, F1),
    F is N * F.
```

More complicated examples occur in the case of trying to search an undirected graph. Suppose that we want a predicate $path(x, y)$ which is to mean that there is a path between x and y, then at first the following seems reasonable:

```
% path(X,Y) is true if there is a sequence
% of edges joining X to Y.

path(X,X).
path(X,Y) :- edge(X,Y).
path(X,Z) :- edge(X,Y), path(Y,Z).
```

Indeed in a directed graph without cycles the program works just fine, but with a undirected graph where both $edge(a, b)$ and $edge(b, a)$ will be true the program generates cycles and runs round and round them. Thus it is necessary to keep track of where one has been if the program is to terminate.

This serves as an example of the fact that in spite of the fact that prolog has a declarative model it is essential to understand the order in which prolog does things if one is to write programs that work correctly. The program above is logically correct but practically incorrect. The most awkward manifestation of this in prolog is the cut.

The cut (!) has the effect of pruning the search tree of a prolog program. Since it is not a logical predicate it can change the behaviour of a program. Following Sterling and Shapiro [92] it is useful to make the following distinction.

- A *green* cut is one which does not change the meaning of the program.

- A *red* cut is one which changes the meaning of the program.

The use of the word 'meaning' requires some justification. It is convenient to define meaning functionally so that two prolog programs that behave identically on the same input have the same meaning. If there is input that causes the two programs to behave differently then we say they have different meanings. Green cuts are usually used for efficiency. We have the following examples,

```
% Green cut.
minimum(X,Y,X) :- X <= Y, !.
minimum(X,Y,Y) :- X > Y, !.


% Red cut.
minimum(X,Y,X) :- X <= Y, !.
minimum(X,Y,Y).
```

In the second program we will succeed with minimum(2,3,3), which we clearly would not want to do!

4.3.2   Prolog Techniques

Prolog's built-in pattern matcher is capable of more than the unification required to make the inference engine work. By assigning priorities to operators it is able to treat single terms as compound ones. This can on occasion be carried too far but it serves as useful syntactic sugar in many cases. We give a couple of examples here.

The 'standard' prolog version of append

```
% append(L1, L2, L3)
% L3 is the concatenation of L1 and L2.

append([], L, L).

append([X|L1], L2, [X|L3]) :- append(L1, L2, L3).
```

is expensive in that it recurses down the first list. Difference lists provide a way to avoid this. When a list L is represented as a difference list, the idea is that it is viewed as the initial segment of some larger list D. The list is then specified as the difference between the big list D and some list $D1$ that starts immediately after L in D. Rather than writing L as the pair $(D, D1)$ we can use the operator $/$, writing $D/D1$ for L. With this formalism we get a new version of append.

```
% concat(L1, L2, L3) the difference list L3
% is the result of concatenating L1 and L2.

concat(D1/D2, D2/D3, D1/D3).
```

In order to be able to use a program like this to concatenate two lists A/B and C/D, (which it will do in constant time) we must be able to unify B and C. In this case the two difference lists are said to be *compatible*. Therefor when using difference lists in order to reap the benefit that the representation can give it is necessary to ensure that the lists one uses are compatible. Such programs require more care from the programmer in setting things up but the care is rewarded. It is a typical example of the way in which an alteration in the view of a data structure can, at a price, reward the programmer.

Another example arises in an implementation of attribute value lists in prolog. It seems desirable to keep all the information on a

particular object in one place. That is to have a single predicate that
links an object to its properties. One learns the benefits of this from
relational database technology. Consider for example the standard
example of course information for a university. A given course will
have a name, a number, a credit value and a list of prerequisites.
There may be more but this will serve for our purpose. If we follow
the relational model we would have a representation somewhat like
the following

```
course(Name, Number, Credits, Prereq1, Prereq2).
```

This limits the number of prerequisites to two, furthermore it leaves
us with a problem in those cases where there are not two prerequisites.
Furthermore we are required to know where in the ordering of arguments each item comes. While all these requirements are desirable
from the point of view of the implementation of a relational database
they impose restrictions on the user that can become burdensome.
It would be nice if we could retrieve information on the basis of the
name of a field rather than its location. To do this without the explicit
introduction of structures into prolog we can use operators.

Operators are used as an adjunct to the prolog pattern matcher
in order to allow one to embed symbols into predicate arguments so
as to cause them to be recognized as compounds. Already the prolog
interpreter recognizes that $A + B$ contains two variables since $+$ is
an operator. The predicate "op" allows one to add to the predefined
operators.

For the current example we introduce an operator ':' with the
predicate op(30, xfx,':') which specifies : to be an operator of low
precedence. The 'xfx' serves to define how ':' associates. We can
then label the fields in the predicate 'course' as follows,

```
course(name:N, number:Num, credits:C, prereqlist:L).
```

This will of course require that we write special predicates to handle
accessing the fields, but we will in fact be able to treat them without
knowing the order in which they appear. Indeed if we have may attributes we could put them in a list whose elements are *attribute:value*
pairs as in

```
course(Name, [number:Num, credits:C, prereqlist:L]).
```

and now it really does not matter in which order the attributes appear.

Of course what we have been doing here is using 'tricks' to try and make prolog do things that are perhaps more natural to other languages. This shows not only the flexibility of prolog but also the effectiveness of the ideas that the other languages have introduced. The attribute value lists of LISP, and the records of Pascal being perhaps the closest motivators for what we did here.

Another tool that has been built into most implementations of prolog also uses difference lists but in a more transparent way. This is the *DCG* or definite clause grammar. While not necessarily suitable for all grammar based applications these program generators provide very useful syntactic sugar in the cases where they can be used. A DCG consists of a set of rewrite rules.

```
a --> b, c, ... , l.
```

This is to be interpreted as saying that a sequence of tokens can be recognised as an instance of 'a' if it can be decomposed into a sequence of subsequences, the first of which can be recognised as a 'b', the second a 'c', and so on up to the last one. A program that recognises a 'b' token list from the beginning of a sequence of tokens S would pass the rest of the sequence to the 'c' recogniser. Thus in prolog

```
% implementation of the grammar rule in prolog

a(S, Sleft) :- b(S, S1),
       c(S1, S2),
       ... ,
       l(Sk, Sleft).
```

This translation is so simple that it can be done directly by the prolog compiler leaving he details of keeping track of the variables to the compiler rather than the programmer. The standard example application to simple declarative sentences in English points up both the virtues and failings of the approach.

Simple DCG for English

```
s --> np, vp.

np --> determiner, noun.
np --> noun.

vp --> verb.
vp --> verb, np.

determiner --> [a].
determiner --> [the].

noun --> [cat].
noun --> [mouse].

verb --> [eats].
```

Which parses 'The cat eats the mouse.' as well as 'A mouse eats a cat', which makes somewhat less sense. As written it would also accept with suitable data 'dogs eats cats'. This can be handled with the introduction of variables into the grammar rules.

```
s --> np(Number), vp(Number).

np(Number) --> determiner(Number), noun(Number).
np(Number) --> noun(Number).

determiner(sing) --> [a].
determiner(_) --> [the].

vp(Number) --> verb(Number), np(Newnumber).
vp(Number) --> verb(Number).

verb(sing) --> [eats].
verb(plural) --> [eat].
```

```
noun(sing) --> [cat].
noun(plural) --> [cats].
noun(sing) --> [dog].
noun(plural) --> [dogs].
noun(sing) --> [mouse].
noun(plural) --> [mice].
```

In addition one can insert prolog code into the righthand side of a rule, this is then embedded into the resulting prolog code generated by the DCG translator.

Before we turn to the use of the different reasoning models in prolog. I want to give one more example of the use of "syntactic sugar" in prolog. This is the ability to define operators. The particular application to the representation of course information is adapted from the book of Gazdar and Mellish [38].

We return to the earlier example of the database on course information. We will represent each course as a directed acyclic graph (DAG) where each arc represents an attribute for the course. The representation that we will give allows both for the possibility that some attributes may not be defined for all courses and for retrieval of them by name. We begin by defining three operators. In prolog syntax we have:

```
?- op(500, xfy, #).
?- op(600,xfx,===).
?- op(600,xfx,ourse).
```

The operator # is used to separate the names of the links in the DAG. The operator === serves as a form of equality, that does not have the usual prolog properties. Its behaviour is determined by the following clauses.

```
X === Y  :-
  value(X,Z),
  value(Y,Z).
```

```
value(Var,Var) :- var(Var), !.
value(Atom,Atom) :- atomic(Atom), !.
value(Dag#Path,Value) :-
  pathval(Dag,Path,Value,_).
```

Pathval is a predicate which retrieves the value of a feature from a DAG while returning the remainder of the DAG. A simple version of pathval which assumes that each DAG is in fact linear and so can be represented as a difference list is given by

```
pathval([Feature#Value1|Dags], Feature, Value2, Dags) :-
    !, Value1 = Value2.
pathval([Dag|Dags1], Feature, Value, [Dag| Dags2]) :-
    pathval(Dags1, Feature, Value, Dags2).
```

In cases where one wants to allow features to have values that are themselves DAGS pathval should be replaced by the following pair of predicates. Unify which determines how two DAGs are to be unified, and pathval itself which extracts the value at the end of a path in the DAG.

```
unify(Dag,Dag) :- !.
unify([Path#Value|Dags1],Dag) :-
  pathval(Dag,Path,Value,Dags2),
  unify(Dags1,Dags2).

pathval(Dag1,Feature#Path,Value,Dags) :-
  !, pathval(Dag1,Feature,Dag2,Dags),
  pathval(Dag2,Path,Value,_).
pathval([Feature#Value1|Dags],Feature,Value2,Dags) :-
  !, unify(Value1,Value2).
pathval([Dag|Dags1],Feature,Value,[Dag|Dags2]) :-
  pathval(Dags1,Feature,Value,Dags2).
```

As written the predicate *value* does not allow for labels on the DAG that are lists. It is however easy to modify the code to permit this.

The behaviour of the operator *ourse* is such as to allow one to enter information on a particular course in the following form.

```
C ourse csc101 :-
C # name === 'Principles of Computer Science',
C # corequisite === mat101,
C # credits === 3,
C # sections === 2.

C ourse csc102 :-
C # name === 'Algorithms and Computers',
C # prerequisite === csc101,
C # credits === 3,
C # sections === 1.
```

Individual values can be retrieved using the following predicate.

```
get_val(C, Path, Val) :- Dag ourse C,
 pathval( Dag, Path, Val, _).
```

In addition it is quite simple to provide a pretty printer that will print the value assigned to a DAG in a nice format.

For this simple example the mechanics are somewhat more than are needed but for more complex examples such as the implementation of PATR grammars in prolog these ideas are quite powerful. When special operators are used in prolog there is often a fine line between uses that clarify by creating a notation that conveys the sense of a program and uses that are merely clever. It seems to me that this example falls into the first of these categories.

4.3.3   Reasoning Structures in Prolog

If we now consider the match between the various knowledge representation methods and prolog we have the following.

Logic Models Given that prolog is based upon a logic programming paradigm it is scarcely surprising that the language captures the logical representation of knowledge easily. There are some difficulties that are consequent upon the introduction of such extra-logical predicates as the cut, and the use of the closed world assumption implied by prolog's negation as failure model.

Networks can be explicitly represented in prolog using a predicate *arc* to assert the existence of links. Furthermore the links can easily be typed by the addition of an extra argument in the definition of arc. On the other hand the process of traversing the network requires that the programmer write the relevant code. The course information example shows how this might be done.

Pattern-Action systems are quite natural in prolog. Indeed very often the process of writing a prolog program involves using just the pattern action technique to give the different clauses for a single predicate. On the other hand prolog's goal directed reasoning may make the forward chaining process of a pattern action system less transparent.

Frames. We remarked earlier that frames can be represented quite easily in prolog. However if one wants to avoid having to keep the slot values in locations that are fixed some overhead is required to be able to retrieve the values. This is in contrast to LISP where the property list mechanism makes this straightforward. However where it is possible to keep track of which argument rpresents a given slot it results in straightforward code. The examples of using links whose ends are named is typical. Here again the ideas from the course information example could be used.

Searching in prolog is easily implemented if a depth first method is used. Breadth first searches and other searches that require the programmer to maintain an agenda can be cumbersome. If the system is not to be forced into frequent garbage collection it will be necessary to store search information in the database using assert and retract. This compromises the uniformity of the prolog approach. Since the information that is asserted is only temporary rather then new knowledge.

Prolog also provides a capability of modeling other reasoning systems through the constuction of meta-interpreters. This is sufficiently important an idea as to warrant its own section.

4.4 Interpreters as Models

An interpreter for a language serves as a model of the language. Indeed one can create an interpreter based upon the computational model of the language. An implementation of prolog can be based upon just such models. The methods by which this can be done are more properly part of a discussion of language implementations. What is important for us in this context is the idea that one can translate a computational model into a physical interpreter.

Both LISP and Prolog are languages for which interpreters can be easily written in the language itself. This bootstrap process was particularly important in the development of lisp. In both lisp and prolog there is the happy consequence that, provided the computational model is not too remote from the one used by the language itself it is possible to write *meta-interpreters* in the language that will implement related computational methods.

Although it would be perfectly possible therefor to write an interpreter for prolog that used a breadth first strategy, one can do much more. One can for example write a forward chaining engine in prolog, or a system that is able to reason using uncertainty. This can be achieved with relatively little effort. Furthermore since the system has an explicit meta-interpreter built for it, the chain of reasoning used to arrive at a conclusion can be explicitly recovered. We can illustrate this with an example drawn from the book of Sterling and Shapiro [92].

The new meta-interpreter will be based upon a predicate *solve*. This is initially a user written predicate that implements a particular reasoning method. It takes one argument *Goal*. Suppose that solve is in fact a conventional backward chaining system which is able to ask the value of certain predicates. We can then build in a tracing facility by modifying solve as follows.

```
solve(Goal) :- solve(Goal, []).

solve(true, Rules).
solve((A,B), Rules) :-
      solve(A, Rules), solve(B, Rules).
solve(A, Rules) :-
```

```
      clause(A,B), solve(B, [rule(A,B)|Rules]).
solve(A, Rules) :-
      askable(A), not known(A),
      ask(A, Answer), respond(Answer, A, Rules).
```

Depenading upon the value of Answer the predicate *respond* will put the information on A into the database. The idea to note here is that as solve goes through the computation it builds a trace of the rules used, which can then be used to provide explanations. In fact respond has a clause

```
respond(why, A, [Rule| Rules]) :-
      display_rule(Rule),
      ask(A, Answer),
      respond(Answer, A, Rules).
```

that provides a reason for asking about the fact A.

Our discussion has centered on prolog, but it is not necessary to restrict oneself to prolog. It is perfectly possible to build an inference system in LISP by defining a function solve and then modifing it so that it can provide the tracing facilities that we described here.

4.5   Non-Standard Logics as Languages

In our earlier discussion of non-standard logics I indicated that one motivation for using such systems was that they can be regarded as extensions of first order logic that are themselves first order. This means that we can use the methods of the previous section to implement some non-standard logics. The alternative of going to a second order logic is not currently viable since computer languages can only deal with quantification over predicates or functions with considerable difficulty.

As an example of the use of a non-standard logic as a language we can consider the case of default reasoning. We recall that one can build default theories based upon the use of default rules.

$$\frac{A(x) : C(x)}{B(x)}$$

Where the interpretation is that $C(x)$ is a consistency check, and that $B(x)$ can be deduced if it $A(x)$ is known and it is consistent to believe $C(x)$. Following the example of a non-standard meta-interpreter we can quite easily build this kind of rule into a prolog system to give a default logic programming system. In fact one can introduce an operator ":" into prolog so that the default rule can be written as

```
B(X)  :- A(X):C(X).
```

Then the special rule for default deduction would take the form

```
default(B(X))  :- clause(B(X), (A(X):C(X))),
                  consistent(C(X), A(X)).

consistent(C(X), A(X)) :- not( (A(X), not(C(X)))).
```

In a similar way one can build meta-interpreters for other non-standard logics, making them into languages. That the resulting system may not be efficient is a legitimate cause for concern. Nevertheless one has a system in which the language can be used. Nor is there anything particularly important about the choice of prolog for the actual implementation language. Indeed the choice of another language might be better depending on the context, we will for example discuss CLP later 5.4.1. It is worth noting however that the prolog programming methodology makes for a particularly smooth transition.

4.6 Object Oriented Programming

Object oriented programming can be summarized as a methodology in which data structures know how to manipulate themselves and are arranged in a hierarchy. The most fully developed implementation of this viewpoint occurs in the language Smalltalk which was developed at Xerox [40]. Smalltalk itself adds to the object oriented view a consistent graphical interface which has had a pervasive influence in the subsequent development of user interfaces. For our current purposes this is less significant than the object oriented approach to programming that is supported by Smalltalk.

Other languages also support the object oriented paradigm. C++ is an object oriented extension of C [94], CLOS provides object oriented capabilities for common LISP and the current version (5.0) of Borland's Turbo Pascal supports some degree of object oriented programming.

4.6.1   The Object Oriented Paradigm

The two basic ingredients of object oriented programming are *data encapsulation* and *inheritance*. Both of these ideas should be familiar from previous discussions. They have not however been viewed in the context of a programming language.

Data encapsulation provides a mechanism for *information hiding*

Put another way it allows data structures to incorporate as part of themselves the methods that are used to manipulate them. When an instance of a given data structure is created all the operations to manipulate it are created along with it. One may think of an object as a frame containing slots that are the allowable operations on the object. The usual word used for this kind of generic notion in the object oriented world is *class*. A class is thus a grouping of both data and operations on the data. The usual examples that are given are such things as stacks, queues, or buffers. I will give an example more closely related to artificial intelligence. It is also closely related to an early example of the object oriented paradigm, namely the turtle geometry of Seymour Papert [1].

A robot can be treated as an object. We may imagine a universe of simple robots in which we can create (and destroy!) new robots at will. If we suppose that the robot lives in a two dimensional world we could define the class robot as having the following attributes

```
CLASS Robot {
        position;
        orientation;
        rotate(angle);
```

```
    advance(distance);
    new(position, orientation);
    destroy;
}
```

Some of these attributes such as *position* report information on the state of the robot. Others such as *rotate* can change the robot's state. In any case these are assumed to be the only legitimate operators on the class robot.

One can then operate in this world by using a sequence of commands. Let us suppose that new returns an identifier that names the robot. So that we can create a new robot 'Carel' (after the Czech writer Carel Capek) by the assignment

```
    Carel = new(origin, north).
```

Carel can then be commanded to move about by a sequence of commands such as

```
    Carel.advance(10);
    Carel.rotate(30);
    Carel.advance(10);
```

We have seen that something like this can be achieved with the property lists of LISP and is also possible in prolog. Although to provide the support for *new* would involve some work, the effect can be managed. The other part of the object paradigm, namely inheritance, is less easily done, (but see Bratko's paper [18] on rapid prototyping in prolog for an implementation of objects in prolog.)

Object oriented programming makes essential use of inheritance, defined as in an IS-A hierarchy, to simplify the construction of types. There is a class hierarchy. At the top of the hierarchy is the class **Object**. Everything inherits from the class object. Every other class is a subclass of some class. Objects are instances of classes.

Classes and objects are different. Objects can be created with some version of a **new** method, and when created in this way they are complete in the sense that all the legal operations on them are defined. Thus 'Carel' is a robot precisely because of the operations that can be performed on him, and these are all the operations. When a new class is created it will require that objects of the new class differ in some way from those of the parent class. This may be either by the introduction of new methods or by adding data. For example a kitchen is a subclass of room, so that in addition to the walls and doors that it inherits from room it will have stoves and sinks. Probably the method clean may well be different as well. Thus the creation of a new class requires the specification of new data or methods, whereas the creation of a new instance requires at most the specification of some predetermined data, exactly what depends on the class.

Thus object oriented programming has a very functional view of the world. Things are what you can do to them. But it also has the hierarchical view that we must explicate a little more. It is convenient to think of the operations on objects in terms of messages that are sent to the object, as we gave 'Carel' commands. When an object receives a message it must determine how to respond to it. If the message involves a method that is defined at the level of the class of which the object is an instance then that is the method used to respond. If however there is no method available at this level the message is passed to the parent class and a method sought there. This process of climbing up the hierarchy continues until either the method is found or until failure occurs at the level of **Object** in which case the system should provide some error handler.

Object oriented languages do not usually permit multiple inheritance, although there are some systems claiming an object oriented approach that do. Such systems must provide disambiguation methods such as we discussed earlier. It is not clear to me that one should provide linguistic support for multiple inheritance, even though natural languages do, at least not until a truly satisfactory theory of ambiguity is available. For the moment Shastri's theory [90] seems to be the best.

4.6.2   Smalltalk

We will illustrate Smaltalk with an example that shows one way in which attribute value lists can be implemented in Smalltalk and shows some of the additional features of the language.

We can represent an attribute value list as a *dictionary*. This is precisely a collection for which items can be stored and retrieved by using a key. Suppose that we want to store information about a particular piece of fruit, an apple say, we can write

```
Apple := Dictionary new
```

This sends the message *new* to the class Dictionary and creates a global variable Apple. (Smalltalk permits both upper and lower case variable names.) We can then add entries to the Apple dictionary as follows.

```
Apple
at: 'color' put: 'red';
at: 'taste' put: 'tart';
at: 'shape' put: 'round;
at: 'variety' put: 'Jonathan'
```

This is a *cascade* of **at: put:** messages to the object Apple. Values can be retrieved with

```
Apple at: 'color'
```

It is also possible to act conditionally depending upon whether an attribute is defined. As in

```
Apple at: 'price' ifAbsent: ['Unknown']
```

Finally it is possible to examine this attribute value list as a whole using

```
Apple inspect
```

This will cause the Smalltalk interpreter to open a window in which the attribute value pairs can be browsed exactly as one might examine a dictionary. This flexible graphic interface is an essential part of the Smalltalk programming environment which makes it very natural to produce systems that have a user interface based upon the use of pop-up menus and mouse clicking.

If we review the other knowledge representation methods as they relate to Smalltalk we find the following representation matches.

Frames. Since each object in Smalltalk is itself a frame or an instance of one we have a very natural representation of frames. Furthermore an IS-A hierarchy comes 'for free'. The browsers supplied by the environment make the inspection of individual frames quite straightforward.

Semantic Networks can be built as objects. It does not seem reasonable to use the existing hierarchy. Rather the network should be treated as a object made up of nodes and links. By providing methods that draw nodes and the arcs between them it is then possible to display the network. Semantic networks are thus less natural then frames in Smalltalk.

Production Systems By building objects that represent rule sets one can add to a Smalltalk system explicit knowledge bases that have specific expertise. The Smalltalk/V[1] system has a class called a logicbrowser which performs exactly this role.

4.7 Imperative Languages: C

The languages that we have discussed thus far have achieved their place in AI programming largely because they are interpreted languages which have lent themselves to an exploratory style of programming. It has been very much part of the enterprise of artificial intelligence that one writes programs and tests them to see if they behave in the way that one expects. This kind of approach seems more suited to languages which are interpreted. In an intelligent system it is to be expected that the input will not always match the expected type. Languages that can cope with this kind of polymorphism seem more natural under these circumstances. Nevertheless there is a place in AI for the paraphernalia of procedural languages.

It is important to understand the advantages that a procedural language can offer. After all these languages are better understood and have received more attention than functional or logic based languages. We can list the major features of procedural languages here.

---

[1]Smalltalk/V is a trademark of Digitalk Inc

- Computational Efficiency

- Strong typing

- Modularity

- Compilation

Of these advantages computational efficiency is probably the one which most justifies the use of a procedural language. Traditional algorithm studies are geared towards determining the best trade off between space and time. Other things being equal faster is better. Since many AI applications are faced by the "combinatorial explosion" problem, they too benefit from faster algorithms.

If we look at the basic methods of AI we find that search plays a central role. Much of the intelligence in a program lies in its choice of search strategy. As the search gets narrower however it becomes more procedural in the sense that the choice of what to do next will not be undone. Arguably therefore when a heuristic method produces an algorithm that is optimal in the sense that search has been minimized it is ripe for procedural implementation.

However it is inappropriate to use just any procedural language unless perhaps the entire problem can be solved in the one language. More than likely the language will have to interface to some less procedural parts. Therefor the language should permit a degree of flexibility that makes this interfacing process easier.

Procedural languages, perhaps more naturally than the other kinds we have discussed, provide for explicit control of memory. At least up to the level of the virtual memory allocated by the system to a process. In addition there will be mechanisms for a dynamic memory allocation in many procedural languages. The user can thus more easily control the placing of some items in close proximity to others. Usually this translates into the ability to build sophisticated data structures that can be used for achieving efficient implementation of certain algorithms. While it may be possible to mimic these structures in the other linguistic paradigms we have discussed one will rarely achieve the same benefits.

A procedural language for use in AI must therefor have sufficient flexibility that it can match the benefits accruing from the polymorphic nature of the interpreted languages. We remarked earlier that an intelligent system must be able to handle data whose type is not determined in advance. This ability is provided by a mechanism such as Ada's[2], use of generics. In ANSI C the use of pointers to voids allows for the construction of polymorphic procedures, since the compiler is required to be able to undo a cast to a void.

Even without these kinds of mechanisms the ability to extend the language with user defined types also provides some of this kind of flexibility. On one level this is more cumbersome than the generic mechanism referred to earlier, but in another sense it fits quite naturally into our context. The use of header files to define the types that will be used plays the role of defining the vocabulary of the language. In this way we can use the same source code for a search program for two different networks by linking it with the header files and other files that handle the information that is specific to the application at hand.

An important consideration in the choice of language has to do with the size of the language. Conceptual simplicity has a considerable appeal. Much of the appeal of Lisp and prolog comes from the fact that at the core of each of these languages there is a simple organizing principle. Moreover there is essentially only one built-in data structure – the list, which is particularly suited to AI. Procedural languages tend to have more constructors built into them. This appears to be a necessary consequence of their efficiency. The C language seems to represent a effective compromise between size and flexibility. It must be said at once that this compromise carries with it a number of potential dangers.

The somewhat cavalier attitude to typing and the ability to write "self-encrypting" code are aspects of C that have, justly, earned criticism from language designers. It does however provide the flexibility that seems to be needed to do some of the things that are useful for AI.

---

[2] Ada is a trademark of the US Department of Defense

4.7.1 C as an AI Language

After the preceding somewhat lengthy and diffuse introduction it seems necessary to provide a more rigorous justification for the use of C as an AI language. In order to be able to do this properly we should identify the kinds of tasks that might arise in an AI program that seem to require procedural implementation.

- Numerical computations

- Rapid access to homogeneous data

- Implementation of Optimized algorithms

At first blush none of these things seems to specifically require that one use C rather than another procedural language. After all FORTRAN enjoys access to a large base of numerical algorithms. Indeed if that is the only task that one wanted from the procedural part of the program then FORTRAN might well be the right choice. What seems to make C particularly appropriate is the fact that subprograms in C are all functions. This means that C shares in part the LISP viewpoint and indeed the prolog one when one recalls that a predicate is merely a boolean function. This ability to see the basic building block of one language (the function in C) in terms of the basic unit of the other language is what makes the relationship of C to AI particularly happy. (See also [19] for another view on blending imperative and relational methods.) That one can match the computational style, at least as seen from outside the program, is a great advantage. Some examples might help.

The following specification of a function could be either for C or prolog

```
find(item, structure, criterion)
/* Sets item to the member of structure  */
/* that satisfies the criterion.         */
/* Returns false if no such item exists. */
```

whereas the following could be either C or Lisp

```
find_item(structure, criterion)
/* Returns the item from structure    */
/* that satisfies criterion.          */
```

This relationship is in fact more than superficial in the case of C. It does indeed correspond to the way in which C programs are written.

Unlike the languages that we have discussed earlier the knowledge representation schemes of chapter 2 have to be constructed explicitly in C using standard data structures methods. Only knowledge that is directly contained in a procedural algorithm is 'naturally' representable in C.

C does of course have arrays available to it. This is an example where one has explicit control over memory allocation that can be used for efficient algorithms. Perhaps the most interesting example of this from the point of view of machine intelligence is the use of hashing to implement attribute value lists. Since this can be construed as a software implementation of associative memory. Note that the other languages that we have discussed provide this more directly although not necessarily as efficiently.

Chapter 5

Changing Representations

This chapter discusses representation change and in particular its effect on the language used to discuss the problem. I will also explore the way in which the choice of language affects the representation of an AI problem.

The AI literature contains several examples that provide different solutions to the same problem. These will provide material for the discussion.

I will describe how one can formally translate between representations and their associated languages. The general principles will then be applied to a number of systems which have been used for problem solving. In particular I will discuss

- Guvernir's Refinement strategy,

- Lauriere's language for combinatorial problems,

- Equation Solving systems,

- The Soar system,

- Analogical Reasoning.

The principal issue to which this chapter addresses itself is that of conversion between representations. This is different from, but not unrelated to, the question of converting an informal representation into a a formal one. Rather we want to deal with reformulation, where one formal representation is converted to another with the goal of using the new representation as a basis for finding the solution.

5.1 Formal Representation Changes

We have seen that describing an AI system, or indeed any system requires both a representation of the system and a language for manipulating the representation. In this section I want to discuss the way in which one can move between different representations. I will begin with a pair of examples drawn from the problem solving domain. This will be followed by a formal description of the process.

5.1.1 Examples of Representation Change

One of the more celebrated examples from the problem solving domain is the *mutilated chess board* problem. One is provided with a chess board from which the pair of diagonally opposed black squares have been removed. In addition one has thirty-one dominoes, each of the size required to cover exactly two of the squares on the board. The problem is to find a way of covering all the squares with the thirty-one dominoes.

While it is possible to determine by a brute force search that this problem has no solution there is an easier way based upon the observation that the problem can be transformed into one which is clearly insoluble. Observe that as each domino is placed upon the board it covers one black square and one white one. Therefore the difference between the number of uncovered white squares and the number of uncovered black squares is an invariant under the placing of a domino on the board. Initially this difference is two. Therefor the problem cannot be solved.

What has been done here is that we have constructed a map from the checkerboard problem into one dealing with two sets of squares, the 30 black squares 32 white ones. In the first problem we can move from one state to another by placing a domino on the board. In the second we remove a square from each set. The fact that we cannot solve the second problem implies that we cannot solve the first since every move on the first problem produces a move on the second. The

1	2	3
8		4
7	6	5

Figure 5.1: An Eight Puzzle Position

converse would not necessarily be true. That is the ability to solve the second problem would not necessarily allow us to solve the first.

The lesson to be drawn from this example is that the existence of a map to a simpler problem can show that no solution to the first problem exists.

Our other example uses one of the many versions of the *sliding tile* puzzles. A common version of this puzzle is the eight puzzle,a state of which is illustrated below.

Several problem solving systems learn to solve this puzzle. Korf [57] gives a complete macro table. **Soar** has been applied to solve the problem [61]. The A^*-algorithm [79] with the 'Manhattan' distance function has also applied. Finally the problem can be represented as a question in group theory. In our context passing to the group representation from the ones used by Korf or in **Soar** requires something slightly different from what happened in the case of the mutilated chess board.

When a problem is formally represented as a group then it must be the case that all the moves are applicable to all the states. On the other hand it is usual to describe the moves on the sliding tile puzzle in terms of the movement of the blank. If a representation based upon this is used there are four moves,

U Moves the blank up one slot,

D Moves the blank down one slot,

L Moves the blank left one slot,

R Moves the blank right one slot.

Evidently there are positions in which some of these moves do not apply. Therefor any change of representation must take into account the possibility of changing the language as well. It is this idea that I want to formalize.

We consider first the case where any operation can be performed in any state. The modifications required when this is not the case will be taken up later.

We may consider a problem as a machine with a state space Q and input set I as follows.

- There is an initial state $\tau : 1 \to Q$,

- a dynamics $\delta : Q \times I \to Q$ and

- an output map $\beta : Q \to Y$.

In most cases of interest the output map β can be considered to be the identity, accordingly we will omit further mention of the output map. A problem instance is then a final state $\phi : 1 \to Q$ and one seeks a sequence of inputs $(x_1, x_2, \ldots, x_k)$ such that $\delta(\tau(1), x_1) = s_1, \delta(s_1, x_2) = s_2, \ldots, \delta(s_i, x_{i+1}) = s_{i+1}, \ldots, \delta(s_{k-1}, x_k) = \phi(1)$. The sequence $(x_1, \ldots, x_k)$ is called a *solution* to the problem. This is sometimes referred to as the *reachability problem*.

In our context we can refer to the input set I as a set of generators for the language of the machine. We will require that one of the inputs corresponds to the null operation or identity transformation. This is necessary for some of our definitions to work properly. Given the assumption that any input is acceptable in any state the language is just I^*, the set of all strings from I.

We saw from the example of the sliding tile puzzle that it is not necessarily the case that all moves are applicable in a given state. So we need to be able to adapt the definition to cope with this. There are two ways in which one can do this. One preserves the totality of the dynamics map the other sacrifices it.

Definition 5.1.1 *A partial problem machine consists on a state space Q consists of a tuple (τ, Q, I, δ) where $\tau : 1 \to Q$ is the initial state, and $\delta : Q \times I \to Q$ is a partial map defining the dynamics.*

Given two inputs x_1 and x_2 and a state s in Q we say that the string $x_1 x_2$ is admissible at s if the composition $\delta(\delta(q, x_1), x_2)$ exists. The set of all strings admissible at the start state $\tau(1)$ is called the language of the problem.

A solution to a problem instance is an admissible string transforming the initial state into the given final state.

The alternative approach is to adjoin to the state space Q an additional absorbing state ϵ representing an error state.

Definition 5.1.2 *A problem machine with error state on a state space Q consists of a tuple $(\tau, Q, \epsilon, I, \delta)$ where $\tau : 1 \to Q$ is the initial state, and $\delta : Q \cup \{\epsilon\} \times I \to Q \cup \{\epsilon\}$ is a map defining the dynamics and such that for all elements of I we have $\delta(\epsilon, x) = \epsilon$.*

It should be apparent that these two definitions describe equivalent objects in that given a problem machine with error state we can obtain a partial machine by removing from the domain of δ the inverse image of the error state. Conversely one can add to a partial machine an error state to obtain a machine with error state.

If we are to talk about change of representation we need to be able to decide when two machines represent the same problem. There is a standard notion of a homomorphism of machines.

Definition 5.1.3 *Let $M_1 = (\tau_1, Q_1, I_1, \delta_1)$ and $M_2 = (\tau_2, Q_2, I_2, \delta_2)$ be two machines then a pair $\phi = (f, \iota)$ where $f : Q_1 \to Q_2$ and $\iota : I_1 \to I_2$ is a homomorphism of the machines if*

$$\delta_2(f(s), \iota(x)) = f(\delta_1(s, x))$$

for all $s \epsilon Q_1$ and all $x \epsilon I_1$, and

$$f(\tau_1(1)) = \tau_2(1)$$

We can extend quite naturally to the case of partial machine by requiring that the target machine M_2 admit at least the operations required to provide images for the operations existing in the domain machine. In other words we must require that in the equation

$$\delta_2(f(s), \iota(x)) = f(\delta_1(s, x))$$

if left hand side exist so does the right hand side.

To make things work for machines with error we must add the condition that

$$f(\epsilon_1) = \epsilon_2$$

Since we can map a non error state into an error state there are homomorphisms between machines with error that do not come from partial machines. Thus although there is one to one correspondence between partial machines and machines with error state the same is not true for homomorphisms.

Whether one uses partial machines or machines with error this kind of homomorphism preserves the language of the machines since the map between the languages is given by a map between the inputs of the machines. Thus we would be unable to use this kind of homomorphism to transform the two representations of the sliding tile puzzle into one another since one is a total machine without error state and the other is partial. What is needed is a mechanism that allows one to transform the language as well as the state space.

In fact one would like to be able to do more. It would be desirable to find changes of representation that simplify the language. The elegant solutions to a problem all seem to share the property that they cast the problem in a way that makes the solution "obvious".

5.2   Weak Isomorphism and Enablement

In this section we describe a notion of homomorphism which because it is weaker than the input-output homomorphism of the previous section allows one to change the language of the machine. It is more convenient to begin by describing it for partial machines.

Definition 5.2.1 *A weak homomorphism* $F : P_1 \rightarrow P_2$ *between two partial machines* $P_1 = (\tau_1, Q_1, I_1, \delta_1)$ *and* $P_2 = (\tau_2, Q_2, I_2, \delta_2)$ *is* *given by a pair of maps $f : Q_1 \to Q_2$ and $g : Q_1 \times I_1 \to I_2$ such that for the map $h : Q_1 \times I_1 \to Q_2 \times I_2$ is defined by the equation*

$$h(s, u) = (f(s), g(s, u))$$

the following diagram commutes:-

$$
\begin{array}{ccc}
\delta_1 : Q_1 \times I_1 & \longrightarrow & Q_1 \\
\downarrow h & & \downarrow f \\
\delta_2 : Q_2 \times I_2 & \longrightarrow & Q_2
\end{array}
$$

This definition adapts to the case of machines with error state as follows.

Definition 5.2.2 *Let $M_1 = (Q_1, I_1, \delta_1, \epsilon_1)$ and $M_2 = (Q_2, I_2, \delta_2, \epsilon_2)$ be a pair of machines with error state. A* **weak homomorphism** *$F : M_1 \to M_2$ is given by a pair of maps*

$$f : (Q_1 \cup \{\epsilon_1\}, \epsilon_1) \to (Q_2 \cup \{\epsilon_2\}, \epsilon_2)$$

and

$$g : (Q_1 \cup \{\epsilon_1\} \times I_1, \epsilon_1 \times I_1) \to I_2.$$

Such that for the map $h : (Q_1 \cup \{\epsilon_1\} \times I_1 \to (Q_2 \cup \{\epsilon_2\} \times I_2$ defined by

$$h(s, i) = (f(s), g(s, i))$$

we have the following commutative diagram.

$$
\begin{array}{ccc}
\delta_1 : Q_1 \times I_1 & \longrightarrow & Q_1 \\
\downarrow h & & \downarrow f \\
\delta_2 : Q_2 \times I_2 & \longrightarrow & Q_2
\end{array}
$$

*By defining f and g as maps of pairs we have ensured that the error
state in the first problem is mapped to that of the second problem.*

This definition allows for considerable flexibility in the production
of maps of problems. In an extreme case it permits us to rename every
operation with the name of the single state to which it applies. As
an example of a weak homomorphism we can consider the following
representation of the five puzzle. There are four inputs

C which moves the blank clockwise around the periphery of the
puzzle,

C^{-1} which moves the blank counter clockwise around the periphery
of the puzzle,

D which moves the blank down, when the blank is in the middle
of the top row, otherwise is an error,

U which moves the blank up, when the blank is in the middle of
the bottom row, otherwise is an error.

We can map the earlier representation to this one by mapping L
to C when the blank is in the top row, and to C^{-1} when it is in
bottom row, R is mapped to C when the blank is in the bottom row
and to C^{-1} when it is in the top row, D maps to C^{-1} when the blank
is in the first column, to D when it is in the second and to C from
the third. Finally U maps to C when the blank is in the first column,
to U from the second column, and to C^{-1} from the last column.
Without wishing to pursue this in too much further detail we point
out that this new representation contains a subproblem generated by
C and C^{-1} which can be used to construct a solution to the puzzle.
For details the reader is referred to the paper by Ranan Banerji [9].
Note also that we can define a weak homomorphism in the reverse
direction.

The foregoing may seem somewhat trite but it can be used to
formalize some fairly basic ideas in problem solving and problem representation. One way to describe the goal of a problem solving system
is that it should decompose problems into simpler ones. If we follow
the idea of a machine then the natural way to compose machines is

to *cascade* them. Informally a cascade of machines is obtained when the output of one machine is connected to the input of another.

Definition 5.2.3 *Let $M_1 = (Q_1, I_1, O_1, \delta_1, \beta_1)$ and $M_2 = (Q_2, I_2, O_2, \delta_2, \beta_2)$ be two machines, where Q denotes the state space, I denotes the input set, O the output, δ the dynamics and β the output function. Then the cascade composition $M_1 \bowtie M_2$ is the machine $(Q_2 \times Q_1, I, O, \delta, \beta)$ where $\eta : I \to I_1$, $\mu : I \times O_1 \to I_2$, and $\gamma : O_1 \times O_2 \to O$ are coding maps that transform the symbols of one machine into those of the other. The state transition and output functions of $M_1 \bowtie M_2$ are given by*

$$\delta((q_2, q_1), \alpha) = (\delta_2(q_2, \mu(x, \beta_1(q_1))), \delta_1(q_1, \eta(\alpha)))$$

$$\beta(q_2, q_1) = \gamma(\beta_2(q_2), \beta_1(q_1))$$

The idea a cascade connection goes back to early work on machines in computer science [12]. It was introduced into problem solving by Benjamin [11]. Note that in the problem solving case the output maps are the identity, which simplifies the above somewhat.

Given a task that is specified as a machine we wish to decompose the task into a cascade of simpler machines. There is the famous theorem of Krohn and Rhodes[59].

Theorem 5.2.4 *Every finite state automaton can be built as a cascade of two-state automata and simple group automata.*

This can be interpreted in our terms as saying that the kind of decomposition that we are looking for is possible. What is not given at this stage is the method for finding the decomposition. We will describe one such approach due to Paul Benjamin, [10]. Its relevance to our overall plan is that the choice of a particular representation, namely the machine, prefers a particular way of approaching the problem, namely the cascade decomposition.

As one examines the dynamics of a cascade:-

$$\delta((q_2, q_1), \alpha) = (\delta_2(q_2, \mu(x, \beta_1(q_1))), \delta_1(q_1, \eta(\alpha)))$$

It will be observed that the action on the first machine can often be embedded in the larger machine, since the second component does

not involve any of the terms with the subscript 2. Benjamin interprets
this as meaning that the moves in machine 1 *enable* those of machine
2. More precisely using the machine with error, if an action ω is not
applicable in a state σ so that $\delta(\sigma, \omega) = \epsilon$ and applying an action ω'
gives a state σ' in which ω is applicable, then we say that ω' enables
ω. Formally:

Definition 5.2.5 ω' *enables* ω *at* σ *written* $\omega' E_\sigma \omega$, *iff* $\delta(\sigma, \omega) = \epsilon$
and $\delta(\sigma, \omega') = \sigma'$ *and* $\delta(\sigma', \omega) \neq \epsilon$.

In order to be able to reason about the effects of more distant
actions, rather than just of the immediate predecessor as enablement
does, Benjamin introduces the notion of partial enablement.

Definition 5.2.6 *Let G denote the set of states in which the action*
ω_n *can be applied. Given the problem (σ_0, ω_n) of applying ω_n and*
sequences $A = \omega_p\, \omega_{p-1} \ldots \omega_1$ and $B = \omega'_q \omega'_{q-1} \ldots \omega'_1$ such that

$$\delta^*(\sigma_0, B) = \sigma' \neg \epsilon G$$

$$\delta^*(\sigma_0, A) = \sigma_p$$

$$\delta^*(\sigma_p, B) = \sigma_n \epsilon G$$

where δ^* is used to indicate the map that describes the execution of a
sequence of operations. If no intermediate state in the above equations
is in G we say that ω_p partially enables ω_n at σ_0, which is written
$\omega_p P_{\sigma_0} \omega_n$.

As an example we can return to our second description of the five
puzzle. In this case the moves C and C^{-1} partially enable U and
D. There is a corresponding cascade decomposition in which the C
moves give rise to a submachine. This cascade has a nice geometric
description that is pointed out by Banerji in [9]. The states of the
five puzzle can be arranged on the faces of a dodecahedron and the
action of C corresponds to the motions within each face. The actions
of U and D move between the faces.

Note however that this elegant geometric description does not
emerge from the first description of the five puzzle. It is necessary
to apply the weak isomorphism that renames the moves to get the

decomposition. Enablement is appropriate as a mechanism for doing this precisely because it involves pairing moves with the state to which they apply. We will call this version of the problem the *universal renaming* of the problem. It is universal because it maps to every representation which can be obtained by renaming some or all of the moves. In the universal renaming each move-state pair is regarded as a distinctly named move, so that the domain of any move consists of a single point.

We can recast Benjamin's theory into the following steps.

1. Transform the problem to its universal renaming.

2. Use partial enablement to construct a hierarchy amongst the moves.

3. Decompose the problem into a cascade of machines based upon this hierarchy.

It is not in fact usually necessary to provide the complete description of the universal renaming. The hierarchy can often be discovered by looking for sequences that can always be applied (as can C and C^{-1} in the five puzzle) and using these as the basis of the first machine in the cascade. We have the following theorem.

Theorem 5.2.7 *Let M be a machine and M_1 a submachine of M such that M_1 is closed under composition of moves. Then there is a renaming of M to M' (that is a weak isomorphism between M and M') such that there is a cascade decomposition of M into $M_2 \bowtie M_1$.*

It is of interest to observe that Korf's notion of *serial decomposability* which is the condition for his method of problem solving using macros to work, is strongly related to this Krohn-Rhodes decomposition of machines.

5.3 Laurière's Problem Solver

In a paper [63] that does not seem to be as widely known as it deserves to be Laurière describes a language and a program for stating and

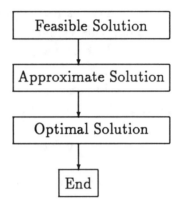

Figure 5.2: The Design of Laurière's Problem Solver

solving combinatorial problems. It is of interest to us here because it is in appearance quite different from most other problem solving systems so that it provides a good example for discussing change of representation. Whereas the other problem solvers use as model the idea of a machine or an action Laurière is guided by a model from operations research. For him a problem is posed as:

> find in a discrete space, a particular point which satisfies
> a given family of conditions.

In describing the method he borrows the language of operations research, so that a problem is solved in three steps. This flow is diagrammed in figure 5.2.

The feasible solution can be viewed as the solution to a relaxed problem, with the approximate solution as an intermediate step in the compression of the solution into the original problem.

The language in which Laurière states his problems is called ALICE. The flavour of ALICE is perhaps best conveyed by giving a specific example of a problem statement in the language. We have chosen to present the fool's disk problem [4]. Recall that in this problem four concentric rings are divided into eight sectors each of which contains an integer. The rings are free to rotate about their common center. The problem is to rotate the discs so that the sum along each

radius of the disc is 12. One reason for choosing this example is that
Laurière's problem solver provides a solution quite different in flavour
from the one that appears in [35] to which we referred in section 3.6.1.
The ALICE description of Fool's disk is:

```
GIVEN   SET  D = INT      1    4           discs
             Q = INT      1    8           octants
        MAT  V ↪ PDT      D    Q Q         octants' values
FIND    FUN  ROT >--> D   Q                rotation
WITH    ∀    J ∈ Q        (    Σ I ∈       D ( V (
        I    1 + (        J    - ROT I     - 1 ) MOD
        8    ) ) = 12)
        ROT  1 = 8
END
```

```
2,1,3,4,2,5,1,3
3,2,3,4,1,3,4,5
3,4,5,3,3,2,2,1
5,1,5,3,4,3,2,4
```

As can be seen the problem statement is in four parts. The first
three parts are introduced by the key words, GIVEN, FIND, and
WITH. The last part occurs after the key word END. The GIVEN
part declares the variable and constants. The FIND part specifies
what is to be found in terms of the variables and constants from
the GIVEN part and a number of language primitives of which FUN
(function) is one. The WITH part specifies the constraints that must
be satisfied. The section following the END specifies the initial condition. ALICE possesses a rich dictionary that allows it to handle a
very diverse set of problems.

Besides this algebraic representation of the problem ALICE also
uses a bipartite graphical scheme to represent information about the
problem and the current state of the search. This is used because
Lauriere interprets a problem in terms of finding a mapping of some
kind (more generally a relation). The two types of nodes in the graph
correspond to the domain and range respectively. So that the desired
mapping then becomes a graph.

ALICE works by trying to satisfy the WITH conditions in some order. (There are several heuristics for ordering these constraints which we will discuss shortly). Thus ALICE uses a relaxation approach in which the goal is enlarged. For example if a (1-1) function between two sets A and B is wanted, the initial bi-partite graph will consist of the sets A and B in which every node in A is joined to every node in B, representing the fact that a priori any element of B could be an image of a given point in A. As the search progresses arcs will be removed from the graph until a graph representing a (1-1) function is obtained.

If we return to the diagram we gave at the beginning of the discussion the feasible solution corresponds to the solution to the extended problem. In many cases the approximate solution is good enough because we are not required to optimize.

Let us now turn to the heuristics that ALICE uses to choose the order in which it attempts to satisfy the constraints. Constraints are ordered by complexity, beginning with the simplest one. (There is a specific algorithm for determining the complexity of a constraint, which works by assigning weights to the symbols and variables that appear in the constraint.) The constraints are then subjected to a reasoning process in the order thus established.

This process has as its goal the simplification and reduction in number of the constraints.For example given the pair of constraints

$$x_2 \geq 0, 0 \leq -4 - x_2 + x_1$$

the system will derive that x_1 must be equal to at least 4.

Having manipulated the constraints ALICE then attempts to satisfy them. This is the process of squeezing the solution to the extended problem down into a solution to the original problem. Constraints are satisfied, using a specific set of rules, in order of increasing complexity. This is based upon a heuristic that seems to be sufficiently prevalent that it is worth stating explicitly.

Heuristic 5.3.1 Principle of Deniability.

When faced with a choice, make the choice that least restricts your future actions.

As an example let us return to the case of Fool's disc and follow the ALICE solution. We quote from p 84 of [63].

> At the time of the first choice, the program considers the constraint which has the largest second member. Taking the seventh one, as $v(1, 7) = 1$, it searches the largest possible value for $(v(2, 1) + (ROT(2))_{mod8})$ which gives $ROT(2) = 7$; then the choice of $ROT(3) = 6$ implies $ROT(4) = 8$ but does not fit. $ROT(3) = 7$ implies $ROT(4) = 4$ and a solution is given.

One of the more interesting things about this method of finding the solution to fool's disc is that is quite different form the solution described earlier in section 3.6.1.

Laurière applies his problem solver to a large number of other problems. A few of which we list here: The Eight Queens problem, Missionaries and Cannibals, Instant Insanity, the Travelling Salesman, graph colouring, resource allocation, scheduling and truck dispatching.

To conclude this overview of Laurière's work and before turning to a more detailed discussion we reproduce two examples of what he calls meta-heuristics. They are closely related to the principle of deniability given above and serve as useful guides in the construction of heuristic problem solvers.

Heuristic 5.3.2 *When making choices*

1. *Make the most informative choice.*

2. *Make the least expensive choice.*

5.3.1   Representation Change in Laurière

One of the more interesting aspects of Laurière's work is that it incorporates an explicit example of representation change. The external interface through the language Alice, of which I shall say more in a moment, is quite distinct from the internal representation in terms of the bipartite graph. Laurière himself refers to the system as a programming language "without instructions". In this sense it is a precursor of the declarative style of programming typified by Prolog.

In this more detailed analysis of Laurière's system I want to discuss the following topics.

- The expressivity of the language ALICE,

- The expressivity of the internal representation, that is the bipartite graph,

- the translation process,

- the search processes of the system.

The Language ALICE

ALICE's dictionary provides in addition to the standard mathematical symbols $+, *, /, -, \Rightarrow, \Leftrightarrow, \neg, >, \geq, <, \leq, =, \neq, \forall, \exists, \epsilon, \Sigma, (,), [,]$ with their usual meanings and logical operators AND, OR, $TRUE$ and $FALSE$, a vocabulary of words for describing functions and sets. The table 5.1 is not complete but gives the essentials for our purpose. The complete table appears in [63].

ALICE is thus able to specify that a problem requires the construction of a function between two finite sets that satisfies conditions given by some algebraic expressions, or the finding of a constant that satisfies some set of equational constraints. We have seen how it can be used to pose the problem of Fool's disk. On the other hand there does not appear to be a provision for structures of variable size. This is because the vectors must have determinate size. In spite of this the system is able to solve problems like the knights tour of a chessboard, because the associated graph is small enough to be described easily in finite terms. It is less clear how effective the system would be in attacking the sliding tile puzzles. (These do not appear as examples of the kinds of problem that ALICE has solved). We shall see that the same limitation reappears in the bipartite graph that is the internal representation of a problem.

The constraints that can appear in an ALICE problem are divided into four types

ALICE's dictionary

Word	Meaning
ALL	Search all solutions
BIJ	Bijection
CIR	Circuit in a network
CAR	Cardinality of a set
COA	Vector with alphanumeric coordinates
COE	Vector with numeric coefficients
CSI	Constants
DIS	Disjunctions
FIND	Key word indicating what is to be found
FMU	Relation between two sets
FUN	Function between two sets
INC	Included in $\subseteq$
INJ	Injection
INT	Closed interval of integers
INS	Set intersection
MAT	Matrix
MAX	Maximum
MIN	Minimum
PAT	Path
PDT	Cartesian Product
SBS	subset
SET	set
SUJ	surjection
TRE	tree
UNI	Set union
$\mapsto$	To define domain and range of a function
$\rightarrow$	Rewrites to

Table 5.1: The ALICE Language: A Partial Listing

1. structure conditions, such as those that a map be a bijection;

2. simple algebraic conditions that involve a maximum of two unknowns;

3. other algebraic constraints with explicit unknowns;

4. other constraints.

An example of a constraint of the last type is a requirement that
if the sought for function maps i to j then some condition $Q(i,j)$ be
true. These kinds of constraints turn up in scheduling problems.

These constraints types are adequate to permit one to deal with
boolean functions as well as with numerical ones.

Finally ALICE is able to state problems in which the question is
one of optimization. This is a clear mark of the operations research
motivation that appears frequntly in the paper. While optimization is
clearly an important issue in Artificial Intelligence I do not intend to
discuss it here. Thus my discussion of Laurière's system will concentrate on the finding of feasible solutions rather than the optimization
phase of the search.

The Bi-Partite graph

When the system reads in a problem description written in ALICE
it begins by translating this description in a formal way into the
internal representation. During the resolution of the problem more
and more of the formal description of the problem is transformed into
this internal representation until finally all the ALICE description has
been incorporated.

The basis of the internal description is the use of a bipartite graph
based upon a pair of finite sets $\mathcal{D}$, the domain set, and $\mathcal{A}$, the range
set, with arrows between them to represent a function. In addition
to this standard representation there are the following features.

- *Cliques* in the domain set of the function, used to represent the
  requirements that a map be an injection or bijection.

- Maximum and Minimum degrees for the nodes in the range set, used to keep track of the number of elements that may appear in the preimage of an element in the range,

- For each node in both $\mathcal{D}$ and $\mathcal{A}$ as well as for every arrow between the two sets a value can be assigned corresponding to some constraint or the objective function.

All the constraints involving at most two variables can be incorporated directly into this graph. So that all information given by the constraints of the first two type listed earlier can be assumed to be so represented. The remaining constraints are retained, but as we shall see in a rewritten form. They are used to guide the search.

Before we proceed to the rewrite rules, let us consider the expressivity of this graphical representation. As can be seen the system, at least as built by Laurière, contains now an explicit restriction to graphs which can be statically represented. There does not seem to be a mechanism that permits the system to deal easily with graphs whose size, or rather number of nodes, cannot be determined in advance. Thus any problem in which it is desirable to avoid listing all the nodes of a graph will not fit simply into the ALICE framework. Note that the restriction is imposed not by ALICE itself but by the internal representation.

To return to the remaining constraints and the rewrite rules. After the construction of the inner graphs the remaining constraints are analysed and standardized. The rewrite rules are applied in such a way that when a rule applies it must be used and the old version of the constraint is forgotten. We will not reproduce the rules here. It is enough to observe that they cover such matters as explicit ordering of arithmetical operations.

During the processing of the rules it may be possible to make further modifications of the graph. These are incorporated as they are found. After this first pass through the constraints a complexity is assigned to each constraint. This is done through the use of an explicit algorithm in which each variable receives a weight of one, $*$ receives a weight of one also, $=$ has weight zero, $\leq$ has weight 3, and any other principal connective has weight 7. There is a tie breaking algorithm so that the constraints can be linearly ordered.

The constraints are then further processed to determine additional information from simple deductions about inequalities. The system thus uses some simple equational resolution before turning to search.

The Search Process

Once the first two phases have been gone through, that is the establishment of the bipartite graph and the initial processing of the constraints there will remain constraints that are unsatisfied. At this point is is necessary to search for a feasible solution. The choices that the system makes are equivalent to adding an additional constraint. This kind of search is what we have elsewhere referred to as a 'restriction' search, only part of the search space is considered. In order to be able to find the additional restrictions the program examines the existing constraints and strengthens one of them. The ways of doing this are, in the order of preference of the system:

1. Assert one of the members of an OR constraint,

2. Choose $i\epsilon D, \alpha_i\epsilon N$, and impose $f(i) < \alpha_i$,

3. Choose $i\epsilon D, \beta_i\epsilon N$, and impose $val(i, f(i)) \le \beta_i$,

4. Choose $j\epsilon A, i\epsilon f^{-1}(j)$ and force $f^{-1}(j) = i$,

5. Choose $i\epsilon D, j\epsilon A$ and force $f(i) = j$.

Each of these strategies restricts the search space in some way. In fact they are all variations of the first one since a constraint of the type $f(i)\epsilon[k, l]$ is equivalent to $f(i) = k$ OR $f(i) = k+1 \ldots f(i) = l$.

Within each category from the above list there may be several choices available to the system. This requires that the system have a method for selecting the first one to try. In the case of the first strategy the heuristic is to choose the OR constraint with the lowest complexity, this has the effect of making the greatest possible reduction in the search space.

The criteria in the case of the remaining strategies are more complicated. Remember that the goal is to find a graph that satisfies a set of conditions. The approach is to do this by exploring how each node must be linked to the rest. There for in constructing a search one has to determine which node $i \epsilon \mathcal{D}$ and its links should be explored first (and where called for a similar choice must be made of a node from $\mathcal{A}$). Laurière lists eight criteria for each node type. I will not reproduce the list here. Rather I will describe what appears to be the philosophy behind the ordering.

The first criterion for the choice of a node from $\mathcal{D}$ is to choose the one with the minimum of possible images. This is typical in that the choice that is made is in some sense the one that is most nearly made already. It leaves the largest number of choices still open. It is also the easiest choice to keep track of, in that there are few alternatives. Thus it is inexpensive whilst also likely to give some useful information quickly. Thus it conforms to the two heuristics described earlier.

Finally the system can in certain cases resort to exhaustive search. Specifically it does this in two cases

1. Local Exhaustive Search, when a constraint is simple enough so that all the alternative can be explored,

2. Global Exhaustive search, when the problem has been reduced to one that is simple enough to be explored completely. There is no point in using a sophisticated argument to deal with simple cases.

Laurère's system is remarkable for it effectiveness. It solves a large number of standard problems quite efficiently. Yet it does so without any problem specific knowledge. Its ability to do so seems to be a consequence of the way in which the two representations used by the system interact. In those cases where after the constraints have been processed it turns out that the graph is small enough to be searched exhaustively it does so. On the other hand when this is not possible it uses the search strategies to select the subgraphs which it will search first. These criteria use the constraints that have not yet been incorporated into the graph, precisely because they are of a form that makes their translation difficult. On the other hand they are of a form that selects subgraphs easily. As we have seen the aim of problem decomposition (and Laurière himself makes this point explicitly) is to reduce complexity of a product $\gamma_1 \gamma_2$ to of a sum $\gamma_1 + \gamma_2$.

Since Laurière's systems uses some simple equation manipulations
it is worth while to consider equation solving systems in their own
right.

5.4   Resolution of Equations

The first time one sees it the analogy between the resolution method
of deduction and the elimination of variables is quite striking. In
essence of course resolution is an elimination of variables in a field of
characteristic two. With this insight and the example of Laurière's
problem solver it is natural to ask for systems that reason as easily
with equations as logic programming systems are able to reason with
Horn clauses. In this section I will discuss the field of *constraint logic
programming* (CLP) in general and Prolog III as a particular example.

5.4.1   Constraint Logic Programming

True logic programming is unable to deal adequately with equality
and inequality. The aim of constraint logic programming (CLP) is to
allow specifications that include equations as well as predicates. As
an example of this consider how one might program the computation
of the Fibonacci series. (This example is taken from [25].) First in
prolog.

```
fib(0,1).
fib(1,1).
fib(N,R):-  N1 is N - 1,
    fib(N1, R1),
    N2 is N - 2,
    fib(N2, R2),
    R is R1 + R2.
```

This predicate fails to be invertible since the 'is' requires that N1
be instantiated. A CLP version of the same program would look as
follows:

```
fib(0,1).
```

```
fib(1,1).
fib(N,R1 + R2) :- N >= 2,
        fib(N-1,R1),
        fib(N-2,R2).
```

Here $N >= 2$ is a constraint. Thus at first sight constraint logic programming looks like prolog with arithmetic added.

An important aspect of constraint logic programming is that a query can yield a set of constraints as its solution. Suppose that we represent the statement that a point (X, Y) is on a circle centered at (A, B) by the predicate.

$$on\_circle(p(X, Y), c(A, B, (X - A)^2, (Y - B)^2)).$$

Then the query

$$? - on\_circle(p(7, 1), C), on\_circle(p(0, 2), C).$$

yields as response the two constraints

$$-2 * B + 14 * A - 46 = 0$$

$$-R^2 + 50 * A^2 - 350 * A + 625 = 0$$

CLP permits the use of q' to represent *not q*. This allows one to avoid the use of *cuts* and the *not* operator which cause problems in prolog.

A Meta-interpreter for CLP

An implementation of a constraint programming language must combine the resolution of logic with resolution of equations. We reproduce here the nucleus of a CLP interpreter written in prolog. This is drawn form [25]. Prolog III uses a different model which we will discuss in the next section.

A rule in CLP can be represented by the prolog rule.

    clause(Head, Body, Constraints)

This corresponds to a CLP rule

Head:- Body {Constraints}.

The procedure *solve* has three parameters

1. The list of goals to be processed,

2. the current set of constraints,

3. the new set of constraints obtained by updating the previous set.

We then have the following meta-leval interpreter:

```
solve([], C,C).
solve([Goal|Remaining_Goals], Previous_C, New_C) :-
      solve(Goal, Previous_C, Temp_C),
      solve(Remaining_Goals, Temp_C, New_C).
solve(Goal, Previous_C, New_C) :-
      clause(Goal, Body, Current_C),
      merge_constraints(Previous_C, Current_C, Temp_C),
      solve(Body, Temp_C, New_C).
```

Clearly the heart of this meta-interpreter is in the procedure *merge_constraints*. A detailed description of the procedure is beyond the scope of this book. The interested reader can consult [3] for an introduction to equational reasoning, the bibilography to which contains an extensive list of further references.

5.4.2 Prolog III

Prolog III is a redesign of prolog which integrates at the unification level

1. The manipulation of trees, including infinite ones and a special treatment of lists,

2. A complete treatment of two valued boolean algebra,

3. a treatment of the operations of addition, subtraction, multiplication by a constant, and the relations $<, \leq, >, \geq$,

4. the general treatment of the relation $\neq$.

The reasoning mechanism of Prolog III is built upon the notion of a *structure*. This is a triple (D, F, R) consisting of a *domain* D, a set F of *operations* and a set R of *relations* on D.

Domains. The domain of any structure is a set. In Prolog III this is taken to be the set of *trees* whose nodes are labeled by one of the following:

1. identifiers,

2. characters,

3. Boolean values 0' and 1',

4. real numbers,

5. special signs $<>^\alpha$, where α is either zero or a positive irrational number.

Real numbers here are intended to mean exactly that, not floating point numbers. All numerical calculations in Prolog III work with rational numbers. An irrational number thus serves somewhat the role of an uninstantiated number.

A tree a whose initial node is labeled by $<>^\alpha$ is called a list and is written

$$< a_1, a_2, \ldots, a_n >^\alpha,$$

where $a_1, \ldots a_n$ is the (possibly empty) sequence of children of a. The superscript α can be omitted whenever it is zero. The *true* lists are those for which α is zero: they are lists of known length. Those in which α is not zero are *improper* lists: they represent finite sequences of trees completed on the right by something of unknown length α. We can concatenate an ordinary list and an arbitrary list as follows

$$< a_1, \ldots, a_m >^0 \cdot < b_1, \ldots, b_n >^\alpha = < a_1, \ldots, n, b_1, \ldots, b_n >^\alpha .$$

Operations Let D^n denote as usual the set of n-tuples from D. An n-place operation f is a mapping from a subset E of D^n to D. Λ denotes the empty tuple. Prolog III supports the operations given in table 5.2.

Constants

id	:	$\Lambda \to$ id,
'c'	:	$\Lambda \to$ 'c',
0'	:	$\Lambda \to 0'$,
1'	:	$\Lambda \to 1'$,
q	:	$\lambda \to q$,
$<>^0$	:	$\Lambda \to <>$,
$c_1 \ldots c_m$	:	$\Lambda " c_1 \ldots c_m "$.

Boolean Operations

$\neg$	:	$b_1 \to \neg b_1$
$\wedge$	:	$b_1 b_2 \to b_1 \wedge b_2$,
$\vee$	:	$b_1 b_2 \to b_1 \vee b_2$,
$\supset$	:	$b_1 b_2 \to b_1 \supset b_2$,
$\equiv$	:	$b_1 b_2 \to b_1 \equiv b_2$,

Numerical Operations

$+^1$	:	$r_1 \to +r_1$,
$-^1$	:	$r_1 \to -r_1$,
$+^2$	:	$r_1 r_2 \to r_1 + r_2$,
$-^2$	:	$r_1 r_2 \to r_1 - r_2$,
$q\times$	:	$r_1 \to q \times r_1$,
$/q'$	:	$r_1 \to r_1/q'$,

List Operations

$\|$	:	$l_1 \to\| l_1 \|$,
$<,>^m$	:	$a_1 \ldots a_m \to < a_1, ldots, a_m >$,
$a_1 \ldots a_n \cdot$	:	$l_1 \to < a_1, ldots, a_n > \cdot l_1$.

General Operations

$()^{n+2}$	:	$e_1 a_2 \ldots a_{n+2} \to e_1(a_2, \ldots, a_{n+2})$,
$[]$	:	$e_1 l_2 \to e_1[l_2]$.

Table 5.2: Prolog III Operations

One-place relations

id	:	a_1 : id,
char	:	a_1 : char,
bool	:	a_1 : bool,
num	:	a_1 : num,
irint	:	a_1 : irint,
list	:	a_1 : list,
leaf	:	a_1 : leaf,

Identity relations

$=$	:	$a_1 = a_2$,
$\neq$	:	$a_1 \neq a_2$,

Boolean Relations

$\Rightarrow$	:	$a_1 \Rightarrow a_2$,

Numerical Relations

$<$	:	$a_1 < a_2$,
$>$	:	$a_1 > a_2$,
$\leq$	:	$a_1 \leq a_2$,
$\geq$	:	$a_1 \geq a_2$,

Approximated operations

$/^3$	:	$a_3 \doteq a_1 / a_2$,
$\times^{n+1}$	:	$a_{n+1} \doteq a_1 \times \ldots \times a_n$,
$\bullet^{n+1}$	:	$a_{n+1} \doteq a_1 \bullet \ldots \bullet a_n$.

Table 5.3: Prolog III Relations

Relations. An n-place relation on a domain D is a subset of D^n. Prolog III supports the relations given in table 5.3.

The use of the term approximation in the last three relations is to be interpreted in the following sense. In the case of approximated division $/^3$ a_1, a_2, and a_3 are all assumed to be real with a_2 non-zero, and if at least two are rational then

$$a_3 = a_1/a_2$$

Similarly in the case of multiplication if the sequence $a_1 \ldots a_{n+1}$ contains at least n rational numbers then we have

$$a_{n+1} = a1 \times \ldots \times a_n.$$

The concatenation relation works similarly. Any list b can be written in the form

$$b = a \cdot <>^\alpha .$$

for unique true list a and irrational α. a is called the *prefix* of b and written $\lfloor b \rfloor$. Then approximate concatenation means that either $a_{n+1} = a_1 \cdot \ldots \cdot a_n$ or a_{n+1} is of the form $\lfloor a_1 \cdot \ldots \cdot a_k \rfloor \cdot b$, where b is a arbitrary list and k is the largest integer for which the element $a_1 \cdot \ldots \cdot a_k$ is defined.

A program in Prolog III is a set of *rules*. Each rule has the form

$$t_0 \to t_1 \ldots t_n, S$$

where n can be zero, the t_i's are terms and where S is a (possibly) empty system of constraints.

A query to such a program takes the form

$$t_0, \ldots t_n, S?$$

To see how Prolog III handles such a query we use an automaton to model the reasoning process. The machine starts from the initial state

$$(W, t_0 \ldots t_n, S)$$

where W is the set of variables appearing in the query. The formulae that summarize the execution of the program are as follows

1. $(W, t_0 \ldots t_n, S)$,

2. $s_0 \rightarrow s_1 \ldots s_m, R$,

3. $(W, s_1 \ldots s_m t_1 \ldots t_n, S \cup R \cup \{t_0 = s_0\})$.

The machine therefore tries to instantiate the left hand side of a rule much as in conventional prolog. Thus in making the transition from the first state in the above list to the last additional constraints are added. Specifically the constraints R from the rule that is applied and an additional constraint $\{t_0 = s_0\}$ from the application of the rule.

As an example of a prolog III program we show how approximating concatenation can be used to transform a sequnce of digits into the integer it represents.

$$Value(<>, 0) \rightarrow;$$

$$Value(y, 10m + n) \rightarrow Value(x, m), \{y \doteq x \bullet < n >\};$$

It is worth noting that the list representation allows one to access the last elements of a list as well as the first.

The above description of the inference in Prolog III does not cover the equational resolution. There is a module within the interpreter that does this. It uses a variant of the simplex method.

Prolog III thus merges resolution of equations with resolution as a method of logical inference. The effect is to produce a system that is better able to manage equality and inequality than the logic programming paradigm of prolog alone. Changing the representation of the concept by building an equation module into the interpreter produces a more powerful system. In the next section we turn to another large system for problem solving.

5.5 Representation in Soar

Soar is an impasse driven problem solving system designed as an architecture for general intelligence. A detailed discussion of the system will be reserved for chapter 6. However it is appropriate to insert some material here on the way in which **Soar** represents knowledge, for while Soar does not manage change of representation directly it is able to control its focus.

The basic mechanism of **Soar** is subgoaling. As we shall see the system has available to it a number of ways of choosing a subgoal. At this point we are more concerned with the way in which the memory of the system is structured.

At any point in the search for a solution the system has

- A current goal. This is the subgoal that the system is currently trying to solve.

- A current problem space,

- A current state,

- A current operator, this is an operator that the system is currently trying to apply.

These four items define the *current context*. They are, to use the frame oriented language of [61], the slots of the current context. Each slot contains *objects* which are *augmented* with additional information. This takes the form of an attribute-value pair list and can relate different objects in the systems memory. These objects are called *working memory elements* or **WME**'s for short.

An important aspect of **Soar** is that it is capable of adding to its list of operators, new ones derived during a search. Thus it is important that the current context be rich enough so that all the information necessary for chunking be present at the time when chunking is indicated. In particular there is no limit on the size of the *augmentation* that an object has, and the augmentation can change with time.

Unlike Laurière's system **Soar** does not have a specific way of representing the problem spaces. This is up to the discretion of the programmer. Knowledge in **Soar** is stored as a collection of productions. Some of these are built into the system from the beginning, others are acquired by the process of chunking. **Soar** can be made to exhibit all the weak methods of problem solving by adding search control productions that express knowledge about the task. (A diagram taken from [61] showing the weak methods appears in figure 5.3). For example, given knowledge about how to evaluate the states in a task, and a preference for states whose evaluation functions are higher, leads **Soar** to adopt a hill-climbing strategy.

5.5.1 The Basic Cycle in Soar

In order to gain a better understanding of the way in which **Soar** uses and acquires knowledge it is necessary that I describe the basic cycle used by the system as it explores a problem. This cycle, called a *decision* in the **Soar** literature consists of an *elaboration* phase and a decision procedure.

During the elaboration phase, new objects and augmentations are added to the system based upon the current contents of working memory. This phase proceeds until "quiescence", and may consist of several steps. A typical production used at this stage takes the form

$$If\ C_1\ and\ C_2\ and\dots\ C_m\ then\ add\ A_1,\dots A_n$$

The C_i are conditions that examine the contents of the context stack and of the rest of working memory, while the A_i are *actions* that add augmentations or *preferences* to working memory. An object in working memory can be accessed as long as there exists a chain of augmentations and preference from the context stack to the object.

Preferences indicate whether

- A choice is to be considered: acceptable;

- A choice should be rejected; rejection,

- A choice is better (or worse than) a reference choice; desirable.

The working memory of **Soar** is thus organized in two distinct ways. First there is a stack of contexts any one of which is accessible, second the augmentation lists create a network structure by linking objects together.

When the elaboration phase is over the decision procedure begins. At this stage all the preferences established by the elaboration phase are available to the system and are reviewed. If there is a clear best preference this is then adopted. The heart of **Soar** is contained in the actions to be followed when there is no clear preference. These states are called *impasses*. There are four types

1. **Tie.** This arises when there are multiple most preferred choices with no preference between them,

2. **Conflict** This arises when there are multiple most preferred choices with conflicts between them,

3. **No-change** This arises when there the current value of every slot is unchanged.

4. **Rejection** This arises when the current choice is rejected and there are no preferred choices. Typically this occurs when all the alternatives have been explored and found inadequate.

For each of these impasses **Soar** proceeds by choosing a new subgoal. In the first two more search is needed and a goal is adopted that corresponds to establishing a preference between the competing choices. Thus a new context will be added to the stack. In the case of the no change impasse there are two possibilities

- *For goal, problem space and state roles.* Assume that the next higher state on the context stack is responsible, and reject it on the assumption that some other path to a resolution can be found.

- *For operator role* This can occur for several reasons, the operator can be too complex for the productions to perform directly or it may be incompletely specified. This requires problem specific knowledge for its resolution. On the other hand it may be that the preferred operator cannot be applied because it is inapplicable in the current state. In this case the default strategy is to adopt the goal of making it applicable.

In the case of a rejection impasse, the higher order context in the stack is responsible and must be rejected. It should be noted that this can occur for one of two reasons. Either the higher order goal has failed or it has succeeded. The inability to distinguish between the two cases is a consequence of the design of **Soar**. Specifically, because **Soar** uses a production system architecture, it can test to see if the goal has been reached on every cycle. Therefor it will not be necessary to deal with the case of rejecting a goal because it has succeeded.

5.5.2 The Language of Soar

A primary assumption in the design of **Soar** is that all intelligent activity can be put in the problem space framework. Problem spaces consist of *states* and a set of *operators* that generate new states from existing states. The primary method for reaching the *goal* in a problem space is *search*.

This approach leads to a system in which all the productions are written in the context of a problem space. We can illustrate this with the initialization required to appy **Soar** to the eight puzzle.

EP1: If the current goal is an eight-puzzle goal then make an acceptable preference for eight-puzzle as the problem space.

EP2: If the current goal is an eight-puzzle goal, then augment the goal with a desired state that contains the desired positions of the tiles.

EP3: If the current goal is an eight-puzzle goal and the current problem space is the eight-puzzle and there is no current state, then create an acceptable preference for a new state and augment it with the initial positions of the tiles.

EP4: If the current problem space is eight-puzzle, augment the current problem space with the operators of the eight-puzzle problem space.

EP5: If the current problem space is eight-puzzle and there exists an operator of that problem space that can move a tile into the empty tile of the current state make an acceptable-preference for that operator at the operator slot.

EP6: If the current problem space is eight-puzzle and the current
state matches the desired state of the current goal in each cell,
make a reject preference for the current goal at the goal slot.

The operators for the eight-puzzle are defined using three more
productions, which we shall not reproduce here. They can be found
in [61] on page 31.

In order to perform search **Soar** contains a number of productions which taken together encompass most of the weak methods of
problem solving. Each of these arises from the addition of a small
amount of task dependent knowledge. It was a requirement of the
Soar architecture that the task dependent knowledge be extractable
from the task environment during problem solving. This should happen quickly and easily, without complex analysis. The search strategy
for a particular problem factors into two parts, $S_u + S_m$, where S_u
is the universal subgoaling method described earlier and S_m which
contains the task specific knowledge.

By using this additional knowledge **Soar** is able to implement
many of the *weak methods* of problem solving. Furthermore since
many of these methods share common subgoals and knowledge incre-
ments a hierarchy of weak methods emerges as a consequence. The
discovery of this hierarchy is a direct consequence of the language and
representation used in **Soar**. (for another taxonomy of weak methods see the chapter by the author in "Formal Methods in Artificial
Intelligence:A Sourcebook" [51]) The hierarchy is given in figure 5.3.

The two B^* methods that appear in the hierarchy are not the same
method, rather they are modifications of the methods the appear as
their siblings in the tree in which each state has both an optmistic
and a pessimistic value.

The central line of the hierarchy uses the impasse resolution method
of **Soar** and provides the backbone on which the hierarchy is built.

There are "weak methods" that do not appear in this hierarchy,
specifically breadth-first search, and the variations of best-first search
such as A^*. These methods seem to require a larger amount of search
control knowledge. The state selection space has to keep available
much more information in the form of an ordered list of states. If
it were permissible to augment the current context with the **OPEN**
and **CLOSED** list of states then these methods could be recovered.

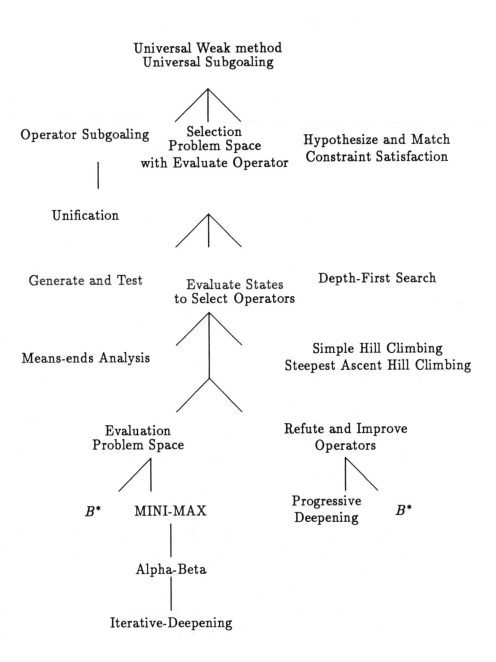

Figure 5.3: The Weak Method Hierarchy

Place Tile 3		
1	2	X
X		X
X	X	3

Place Tile 5		
1	2	3
X		4
5	X	X

Figure 5.4: Symmetric States in the Eight Puzzle

However as we shall see in a moment this would cause problems with chunking.

As has been indicated earlier **Soar** uses chunking as its mechanism for learning. In **Soar**, single-production chunks are built for every subgoal that terminates.

For each goal generated, the architecture maintains a condition list of all data that existed before the goal was created and was accessed during the the goal. Access in this context means that a production that matched it fired. When a goal terminates, the condition list for that goal is used to build the conditions of a chunk. Before the condition list is turned into the chunk condition it is necessary to replace some of the data by variables so that the conditions become tests for object descriptions rather than tests for the specific objects that occurred in the original goal.

One of the consequences of this is that **Soar** can come to recognize symmetries in a problem. This happens for example with the two positions in the eight puzzle shown in figure 5.4.

Soar is capable of recognizing that the solution to the left puzzle contained in the right-hand two rows can be used in the right-hand puzzle in the bottom two rows. It does this in spite of not having been given the symmetry directly.

On the other hand there are problems that arise with **Soar's** chunking mechanism in that it can overgeneralize. The pair of examples from Tic-Tac-toe in figure 5.5 shows how this can occur.

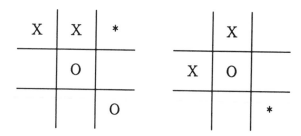

Figure 5.5: Overgeneralization in Tic-Tac-Toe

In the left hand diagram choice of the starred square leads to a victory for **O**. In the right-hand diagram it is an error. This overgeneralization can occur if the fact that the square in the middle of the left hand column is empty fails to be part of the condition of the chunk. If this was not tested in finding the earlier solution it will not be part of the condition.

Soar's production rule based language fits cleanly with its learning method. But by the same token it would be difficult for it to learn strategies that came out of best first type searches.

5.6 Analogical Reasoning

Considering the fact that reasoning by analogy seems to be a popular method of human reasoning it has been relatively little used in the field of Artificial Intelligence. This is all the more surprising since the use of analogy is one of the principal ways in which one might envision inter-task transfer of knowledge taking place. In this section we will review a the early work on analogy contained in a paper by Jaime Carbonell [21] and contribute some remarks on how analogy can be placed in a general framework. In the next section we will discuss the work of Stuart Russell on determinations and analogy [85].

Carbonell discusses a computational model of problem solving by analogy based upon an extension of means end analysis. The central hypothesis (quoted from the reference cited earlier) of the work is the following:

> When encountering a new problem situation, a person is reminded of past situations that bear strong similarity to the present problem (at different levels of abstraction). This type of reminding experience serves to retrieve behaviours that were appropriate in earlier problem solving episodes, wherupon past behaviour is adapted to meet the demands of the current situation.

5.6.1   The Analogy Transform Problem Space

Carbonell's analogical reasoner is based upon the idea of an *analogy transform problem space* which he also calls T-space. This is defined as follows:

- The states in T-space are potential solutions to problems in the original problem space (that is, sequences of states and operators including the initial and final states, plus the path constraints under which these solutions were computed).

- The initial state in the transfrom space is the solution to a similar problem retrieved by the reminding process.

- A goal state in the transform space is the specification of a solution that solves the new problem, satisfying its path constraints.

- An operator in the transform space maps an entire solution sequence into another potential solution sequence. Carbonell lists the following as the most useful such operators

  - General Insertion. Insert a new operator into the sequence.
  - General Deletion. Delete an operator from the sequence.
  - Subsequence Splicing. Splice a solution to a new subproblem into the sequence.
  - Sub-goal preserving substitution. Substitute an operator in the original solution sequence that reduces the same difference.

- Final-Segment Concatenation. Treat the solution sequence as a macro-operator in the original problem space and apply means end analysis to reduce the difference between the old final state and the new final state.

- Initial-Segment Concatenation. Apply the process above to find a path in the original problem space from the new initial state to the old initial state.

- Sequence meshing. Merge the operator sequences of two complementary solution retrieved by the reminding process.

- Operator reordering. Reorder the operators in a solution sequence.

- Parameter Substitution. Substitute the objects to which operators were applied in the retrieved solution by corresponding objects in the new problem specification.

- Solution Sequence truncation. Eliminate unnecessary operators.

- Sequence Inversion. Reverse the operator sequence.

- The *Difference Metric* in the transform space (D_T) is a combination of the difference measures between the initial states (of the retrieved and desired solution sequences), final states, path constraints, and degree of applicability of the retrived solution in the new problem scenario. The values of D_T are 4-vectors.

$$D_T = < D_O(S_{I,1}, S_{I,2}), D_O(S_{F,1}, S_{F,2}),$$

$$D_P(PC_1, PC_2), D_A(SOL_1, SOL_2) >$$

where

- D_O is the difference in the original space.

- D_P computes the difference between the path constraints.

- D_A measures the applicability of the old solution in the new scenario.

- A difference table for indexing the T-operators is needed.

- There are no path constraints in the transform space.

It will be observed that the above description is very much tied to the means-end analysis approach. This is evidenced by the presence of the difference metric and the difference table in the above description of the T-space.

5.6.2   Finding the Analogy

As we know from our own experience the effectiveness of reasoning by analogy is dependent on finding the correct analogy in the first place. Thus as Carbonell points out in [21] in planning a trip from Pittsburgh to New York inter-city train is a usable analogy for air flight whereas the subway is not. Even though in some situations the subway is a better analogy to inter-city trains than airplane would be.

Thus the correct analogy depends upon the goal which is to be achieved. In the context of means-ends analysis the transformation is achieved by a *subgoal preserving substitution* T-operator. In the example above train travel can be substituted for air travel since they both reduce the same difference. In a similar way a smart monkey having observed the experimenter set up the "monkey and bananas" problem would be able to translate the operators used by the experimenter into the corresponding operators used by the monkey.

An analogical reasoner is thus likely to have a series of script-like *pre-solutions* to a number of problems that can serve as initial states in the transformation space.

5.6.3   A Framework for Analogy

In order to give a framework for an analogical reasoner we will give a definition of an analogy. We need a definition that maps one problem into another but it must be less restrictive than that required for a problem morphism which we discussed earlier. It will also be necessary to have some measure of the closeness of an analogy.

We will represent a problem P by the triple (S, Ω, a) and will in fact prefer to consider the associated categorical object $Seq(P)$

consisting of all admissible sequences of operators on P. We can define the category of *instances* of P to be the category $\mathcal{I}(P)$ whose objects are the pairs (s_1, s_2) of states of P, the morphisms in this category consist of the identity and a unique morphism for each pair (s_1, s_2), (s_3, s_4) whenever $s_2 = s_3$. There is a forgetful functor $\mathcal{S}eq(P) \rightarrow \mathcal{I}(P)$. In addition there is a forgetful functor from $\mathcal{S}eq(P)$ to $\mathcal{F}(P)$ the category whose morphisms are the words in the operators of P.

Definition 5.6.1 *A solution to a problem is a right inverse to the functor* $\mathcal{S}eq(P) \rightarrow \mathcal{I}^0(P)$ *where the superscript* 0 *denotes the solvable instances of* P.

An analogy *for a problem* P *consists of a solved problem* P_a *and a pair of functors* $\mathcal{A}: \mathcal{I}(P_a) \rightarrow \mathcal{I}(P)$, $\mathcal{A}^*: \mathcal{S}eq(P_a) \rightarrow \mathcal{F}(P)$.

The solution to P_a composes with the functor $\mathcal{A}^*$ to provide the proposed solution to the given instance of P. An analogy is called *effective* if it can be defined by a functor $\mathcal{S}eq(P_a) \rightarrow \mathcal{S}eq(P)$. In this case a solution to the analogous problem will provide one for P if the image of $\mathcal{A}$ covers $\mathcal{I}^0(P)$, hence the choice of name.

Closeness of the analogy is measured in two ways.

- The degree to which $\mathcal{A}^*$ fails to map into $\mathcal{S}eq(P)$.

- The degree to which the image of $\mathcal{A}$ fails to cover $\mathcal{I}^0(P)$.

Note that since this definition allows some operators to be mapped to the identity there will be operators available in the original problem for which there is no analogy. It remains to describe how this formalism will facilitate the discovery of analogies.

The analogy system needs to be able to "remember" solutions to earlier problems that are of a similar type. It seems that this is best described by a functor

$$\mathcal{I}(P) \rightarrow \mathcal{I}(P_a)$$

which selects the analogous problem P_a and will be inverse to the functor $\mathcal{A}$ of the analogy. The construction of such an functor is evidently going to be problem dependent. For example in the case of the two monkey and bananas problems or the train-plane problem the features that describe the difference between the initial and final states are the same in each case. Indeed this latter seems to be the strongest example. Another example where one could have the same kind of feature equivalence is if one were to recall the blocks world as an analogy to the Tower of Hanoi, since each deals with the position of items in piles.

5.7   Determinations and Analogy

If an analogy is to be effective we must know that the information that we are trying to analogize is relevant. For example if we construct an analogy between a military campaign and an illness. Then we can ask "what is the military equivalence of a vaccination?". How do we know that the structure that we are trying to carry over is effective. Recent work of Stuart Russell [85] addresses this problem. The critical idea is that of a **determination**.

Determination seeks to encapsulate the idea of relevance. The idea is that if a property P is relevant to Q then changing the value of P should influence the value of Q and that knowledge about the value of P should restrict the value of Q in some way. More formally we can proceed as follows.

Define $\mathbf{X}$ to be the set $\{x : P(x)\}$, the set of objects satisfying P. Let $N =\mid X \mid$, the number of such objects. Define $d(P,Q)$ to be the *degree of relevance* using the following formula

$$d(P,Q) = \frac{1}{N(N-1)} \sum_{X_i \epsilon \mathbf{X}} \mid \{X_j : X_j \epsilon (X - X_i) \wedge \exists Z[Q(X_i, Z) \wedge Q(X_j, Z)]\} \mid$$

This gives the average over all X satisfying P, of the proportion of other X's with the same value of Q. Given a binary predicate $P(x,y)$ we can define a unary predicate $P_W(x) \Leftrightarrow P(x,W)$ for each W such that, for some X, $P(X,W)$ holds. We can then write the determination for P as the average of all the determination factors of the P_W's:

$$d(P,Q) = \frac{\sum_W d(P_W, Q)}{\mid \{y : \exists x P(x,y)\} \mid}$$

These measures give an empirical probability that a solution for
Q, obtained by analogy on the basis of a similarity P will be correct.
Russell next introduces the notion of total determination denoted by
$\succ$

$$P(x, y) \succ Q(x, z) \; iff$$
$$\forall wyz[P(w,y) \wedge Q(w,z) \Longrightarrow \forall x[P(x,y) \Rightarrow Q(x,z)]]$$

The basic theorem for sound analogy is as follows.

Theorem 5.7.1

$$(P(x,y) \succ Q(x,z)) \wedge P(S,A) \wedge P(T,A) \wedge Q(S,B) \Longrightarrow Q(T,B).$$

The contents of this theorem is that total determination is a sufficient condition for analogy to work.

In contrast to the ideas of the previous section the material for
the analogy is represented in terms of predicates. Conjunction of
predicates is commutative whereas the categorical approach works
with moves and their compositions which may not be commutative.
Taking this into account the condition for a sound analogy in the
theorem can be seen as equivalent to the categorical conditions that
we gave earlier.

Chapter 6

Large Scale Models

In this chapter I will discuss the ways in which large systems can be constructed using the ideas that have been introduced earlier. I will discuss two systems in some detail. The first is the **Soar** system which we have already met. The other is the Cyc system of Douglas Lenat.

I hope to show that in each case there is a central organising principle based upon the interaction between the representation of knowledge and the language.

It is often claimed that building large scale intelligent systems is qualitatively as well as quantitatively different from building small ones. Their size makes them necessarily complex. Perhaps the most persuasive advocate of this position is Doug Lenat in his introduction to the "Cyc" system [66], although this is by no means the only place where he makes the argument, nor is he the only one to do so. On the other hand as I hope to show even large systems must have some organizing principles that make them "graspable".

Before discussing the large scale systems in detail let us consider the aspects that can be expected to make them different from smaller scale systems.

Perhaps the most obvious shortcoming of small systems is their "brittleness". This is the phenomenon of over-specialization. An expert system may be very good at diagnosis in a limited domain but will fail completely the moment the boundaries of the domain are reached. This is in marked distinction to the more desirable characteristic of "graceful degradation" where the system might still produce useful results beyond its area of expertise. The most likely explanations for brittleness in a system are the following:

- Insufficient knowledge beyond a very narrow domain,

- Choice of a class of representation whose extent is circumscribed,

- Restricted reasoning abilities consequent upon lack of expressivity of the system's language.

Thus an expert system to diagnose faults in internal combustion engines is unable to diagnose faults in electric motors, even though both devices can be used for powering vehicles – a knowledge deficiency. Laurière's system is unable to handle problems in which the size of the graph cannot be determined – a representation deficiency. **Soar** does not handle certain kinds of search because its language does not permit it to talk about an agenda – a language deficiency.

In constructing a large system it therefor seems inevitable that the system will have available

- A "large" knowledge base,

- A flexible representation system

- Several methods of reasoning and a language system capable of using them.

One of the threads that seems to run through all Artificial Intelligence work is the problem of expressing knowledge 'at the correct level'. Introspection of our own experience tells us that there are some things that we 'just know' whereas as there are others where we have to reason them out. On occasions it is even the case that the things that we 'know' just don't work and we must resort to 'figuring it out'. An every day example of this comes in the field of natural language understanding. Usually we do not have to think too much to understand a sentence, but from time to time we will be faced with one that is less transparent to us and we must spend time analyzing it. Garden path sentence such as

The horse raced past the barn fell.

provide particularly apt example here, (especially for those of us who afflicted with an arcane vocabulary recognize 'fell' as a possible adjective.)

These two kinds of knowledge seem to be quite fundamental for all intelligence. Some knowledge has the form of compiled chunks which are readily retrievable for use by the agent, other knowledge is deeper and must be 'ferreted out" when the compiled knowledge fails. The point of this argument is that any large scale intelligent system can be expected to incorporate both kinds of knowledge, but must do so in a coherent way. So that by understanding the function of a motor as a power device we may be able to reason about what might be wrong with an electric mower, even though previously we were only familiar with mowers powered by an internal combustion engine. Both the actual systems that we will discuss in this chapter confront this issue quite directly: rightly so for it seems to be one of the central issues of intelligence.

Besides discussing these specific large systems we will also discuss two organizing principles for large systems. One is the blackboard system which models the cooperation of experts and the other is the notion of hypertext. This latter offers new ways of structuring large knowledge bases and powerful metaphors for constructing interfaces to them.

6.1 Soar as a Large System

In describing the genesis of **Soar** (see the preface in [61]) Alan Newell explains that it had become clear to him and others working with him at the time that it was time to build a production system that would have a large number of productions. The original target was one thousand. Thus **Soar** was always intended as a large system. Furthermore, in the words of Alan Newell "the system was to be grown not programmed". Indeed the original name for the system was "The Instructible Production System". It was only later with the advent of chunking that the system became a learning one as well.

6.1.1   Focus in Soar

One of the major consequences of the decision to "grow" **Soar** is
that as a production system it is impossible to make the assumption
that the agent adding a new production knows all, or indeed even
any, of the other productions in the system. This constraint which is
eventually enforced by the limitation that one cannot consult all of
the memory of the system is further enforced by the architecture of
Soar.

This raises the important issue of *focus*. How does an intelligent
agent choose what it is to focus on at any given point in time? A
completely procedural solution to a problem resolves this problem by,
in a sense, wishing it away. It just "knows" what to do next, that
is why it is a procedural solution. On the other hand declarative
systems hide the focus problem within their execution process. **Soar**
deals with the problem by confronting it head on. The *current context*
is exactly the "focus" of the system. By making the task space an
explicit part of the current context **Soar** is able to use productions
to determine when the current task should be modified. In fact this
is the heart of **Soar**.

If we recall the description of the eight-puzzle in **Soar** we had a
series of productions that were used to establish the initial context for
the problem. (These are listed on page 157). The rules that change
the context are exactly what make **Soar** into an "impasse driven"
system, in that when no further progress can be made with the current
problem space a new problem space must be found. Furthermore the
system retains augmentations that may link the current context to
previously instantiated contexts.

Change of focus in **Soar** occurs then in response either to an
impasse or could take place as a consequence of a specific production
rule directing such a change. This will happen for example when the
system has learned a chunk that directs such a switch in focus. The
significance of this is that **Soar** can learn from experience, but unless
it is explicitly instructed to do so will not switch to a context that is
not a subgoal of one of the contexts in its working memory. With this
in mind let us review what is necessary for a user of **Soar** to write an
application using the system.

6.1.2 Applications in Soar

The minimal set of productions that must be supplied by the user must include task-implementation knowledge.

1. Knowledge that defines the initial problem space.

2. Knowledge that defines the initial state.

3. Knowledge about the goal state and how it can be recognized.

4. Knowledge about operators that can transform states.

5. Knowledge about how to apply operators to change the states.

The **Soar** manual uses the term 'propose an operator' this is because in the first phase of the decision cycle the productions determine preferences as to what should be done. The proposal language accords with this.

In addition there may be productions that relate to search control knowledge.

1. Knowledge about assigning evaluations to states.

2. Knowledge about assigning preferences to states or operators.

Soar is thus more of an inference engine with learning capabilities. Other than its architecture and impasse driven inference system it is not possessed of any knowledge other than that the user gives to it. It is for this reason that Soar is described as a universal weak method.

In structuring a **Soar** application it is important to take into account both the architecture and learning mechanism of the system. Since the system uses subgoaling as its "universal mechanism" for impasse resolution the productions that are supplied to the system should facilitate the hierarchical decomposition of tasks. An example of this occurs in the case of the **Soar** implementation of the computer configuration system **R1**. Then the performance of the system is traced it is found that the system produces as subgoals the natural hierarchical decomposition,

backplane → module board → module board slot.

6.1.3   Representation in Soar

In order to make chunking more effective the representation and pro-ductions should be chosen so that the pre-conditions for the chunk can be made sufficiently general. When a chunk is formed the system uses a process called *backtracing*. Whenever a production produces a subgoal result, backtracing examines the production trace, to see which working elements were matched. If a matched working memory element is linked to a supercontext, it is included in the chunk's con-ditions. If it is not so linked, then backtracing recursively examines the trace of the production that created it.

The identifiers of actual objects in the conditions of the chunk must be replaced by variables if chunking is to have any capability of transfer. The task representation, which is determined by the user, will therefor have an effect upon both the efficiency of the subgoaling mechanism and the value of the chunking process.

As an example of the kind of thing that can be done we review [60] the way in which **Soar** learns Korf's solution [57] to the eight-puzzle using macros. To do this Soar requires two problem spaces. The first contains the normal eight-puzzle operators and the second contains operators corresponding to the serial decomposition of the puzzle. Thus the operators of the second problem space are the macros that must be found. Problem solving starts in this second problem space with an attempt to apply a series of the high-level operators. These operators must, however, be implemented in the normal eight-puzzle problem space. The chunking mechanism used by Soar means that the resulting macros can be quite efficiently encoded because the system automatically ignores the positions of tiles that have not yet been placed since they are in fact irrelevant for the macro.

The choice of representation is thus seen to be critical for both the efficiency of execution and learning in **Soar**. Although usable chunks can be created even in the absence of a good representation. By way of example [60] describes (page 55) the efficiency of two different rep-resentations of the eight-puzzle for the encoding of the task space and the eventual number of productions required to encode the macros.

As a problem solving system **Soar** relieves the user of the diffi-culties of encoding basic search methods and learning, leaving only the task specific knowledge. Current versions of Soar are written in common lisp, making it quite portable. The current version provides facilities for following the learning process and otherwise tracing the execution of the system.

Soar manages the problem of deep and shallow knowledge through its chunking mechanism. The chunks represent compiled partial solutions and will be tried at the same time as the 'deeper' base level Soar mechanisms. Thus if there is no 'deep' knowledge available the system can resort to its own version of first principles.

6.1.4   Expensive Chunks in Soar

In a recent paper [96] Tambe, Newell and Rosenbloom discuss a problem that can arise from Soar's chunking mechanism that is relevant to the whole question of language and representation. The essence of the difficulty is that as Soar creates more chunks of knowledge the time spent on the matching of chunks can come to consume an ever increasing proportion of each elaboration cycle. In the cited reference the authors present a solution to the problem that is based upon restricting the expressivity of the language used to describe the problem. Since what is at issue here is precisely a trade off between language capabilities and performance it is worth our while to pursue the matter further.

A chunk in Soar takes the form

```
IF A and B and C and D   then D.
```

In matching a chunk such as this Soar will generate a search tree that requires it to instantiate tokens to represent the bindings of the variables that occur in the chunk. Thus an attempt to match a chunk like the one above will require that tokens be generated for the variables that occur in each of the components A, B, C, and D. There are two factors that determine the cost of such a search. These are the depth of the search tree, corresponding to the number of components in the chunk, and the "bushiness" of the tree which is determined by the number of ways in which it is possible to match the variables occurring in each component. This phenomenon occurs also in the prolog pattern matching engine, and for exactly the same reasons.

The height of the search tree is called the *footprint* of the chunk. Although the footprint of a chunk can have a large impact on the cost of matching a chunk it turns out to be a relatively minor part of the cost. The branching of the search tree has the greatest effect. In particular if the number of possible branches is kept small (that is usually equal to one) then matching can be made almost linear in the depth of the tree, whereas significant branching will make for exponential cost.

The source of branching in the search tree is the presence of *multi-attributes*. This refers to a set of Working Memory Elements (WME) with multiple values for a fixed class. The key to eliminating branching therefor lies in the elimination of multi-attribute elements. We can illustrate this with the example of the eight puzzle. If we have a representation in which *move* means sliding and tile adjacent to the blank into the blank slot there can be as many as four matches in a given state leading to a large branching factor. On the other hand if we have four different moves corresponding to the four directions in which the blank can be moved. Then for each token to be matched in a WME the direction of the move will be already expressed leaving only one branch.

The avoidance of multi-attributes in WME's makes the language less expressive and requires that the representation be designed so as not to require multi-attribute WME's. Tambe et al. describe experimental results in which they have done such removal and obtained speed up.

That the use of a less expressive language should be desirable seems at first somewhat counterintuitive. In fact what is happening is that the language has been tailored to match a specific reasoning process. Compactness of representation has been traded for speed. It suggests that if one could automate the translation to unique-attribute systems it might be possible to have the best of both worlds. A visible compact representation on top of an invisible fast one.

6.2 The Cyc System

The **Cyc** system seeks quite directly to deal with the problem of brittleness in intelligent systems. The approach is based on the observation that as intelligent agents, humans are not brittle because they have a very large body of knowledge available to them. In the language that we used earlier a human being can fall back on reasoning from "first principles" when she does not have the specific "compiled" knowledge that is required to solve a problem.

The builders of the Cyc system set out to build a system that would be possessed of the amount of common sense knowledge that is assumed of the reader of a one volume desk encyclopedia. What is perhaps of primary interest to us about Cyc is the fact that the designers found it necessary to have two ways of representing knowledge. We shall therefor cast our discussion around the reasons for this outcome.

6.2.1 Overview of Cyc

It is clear that any knowledge representation system must at some level have recourse to the use of some primitive notions in terms of which the rest of the knowledge in the system can be defined. The problem lies in determining what the appropriate primitive for the system should be. The solution adopted by the designers of Cyc can best be understood in terms of what Lenat calls the "Representation Trap".

The most economical way to describe the representation trap is to say that it is the inevitable consequence of storing knowledge at a level which is too specific. We saw this phenomenon earlier in the case of Shastri's work on semantic models where he concluded that it is necessary to store knowledge at the most general possible level. In human terms we do this when we store our knowledge of how to drive a car in such a way that after a brief examination of the interior of a car we can usually drive the thing even if it is of a make which we may never have driven before (or for that matter even heard of.) This argues that our knowledge of car driving is not stored in the form

- How to drive a Ford;

- How to drive a Peugot;

- How to drive a Honda.

rather we have a more generic formulation " How to drive a car with automatic transmission"; although we may also keep special information about the peculiarities of a particular manufacturer or even a specific vehicle.

From this is is a fairly natural step to observe that people have already addressed the problem of primitive knowledge representation in at least two places: encyclopedias and dictionaries (at least those dictionaries designed to tell us what words mean.) When we use an encyclopedia we are aided by our knowledge of what kinds of things are likely to appear as the titles of entries. Something that we learn early in life. Furthermore the items are arranged sequentially so that organization is not a problem. Finally there is the cross-referencing system that enables us to navigate within the book when our first guess is not quite right.

Cyc's knowledge base is designed to provide the common sense knowledge that is needed to understand an encyclopedia or a newspaper. Initially the knowledge base is constructed manually but it is hoped that eventually a natural language interface will allow additions to the knowldege base to be made automatically. In the initial stages however it was deemed necessary to work with a system for manual entry. Thus an important aspect of the construction of Cyc is the determination of the underlying common sense assumed by writers of encyclopedia articles and newspapers.

Since Cyc is a large scale project it had to be designed so that the knowledge base can be worked on by several people at one time. As a practical matter the system must be architected to make this possible. The system has an interface that allows the user to enter new knowledge into the system. This is supported on a local machine which is connected to a central knowledge server. In the event that a user enters data that conflicts with other information known to the system Cyc mediates a discussion that tries to resolve the problem.

6.2.2   The CycL Representation Language

Cyc uses frames as its fundamental method for representing knowledge. The values of each slot in the frame form a set. Thus an example frame (the word *unit* is used interchangeably with frame in the Cyc literature,) would be:


```
Pennsylvania
   capital: (Harrisburg)
   population: (18,000,000)
   stateOf: (UnitedStatesOfAmerica)
   majorCities: (Philadelphia Pittsburgh Scranton)
```


Note that each slot value is a set, even if it is a singleton. The following conventions are used for referring to units, slots, and values.

$$u \; = \; \text{unit}$$
$$s \; = \; \text{slot}$$
$$v \; = \; \text{value}$$
$$v1 \; = \; \text{one entry in the value set}$$

Notationally one can write $s(u, v1)$ or $u.s.v1$ to mean that $v1$ is a value in the s slot of the unit u.

There are different kinds of frames that exist in Cyc. Most of them are *normal units* that represent real-world concepts. In addition there are other units, *SlotUnits*, *SeeUnits*, and *SlotEntryDetails*.

SlotUnits are frames that represent types of slots. They contain information about the slot. For example

```
majorCities
   instanceOf: (Slot)
   inverse: (majorCityof)
   makesSenseFor: (GeopoliticalRegion)
   entryIsA: (City)
   specSlots: ()
   slotConstraints:
```


SeeUnits provide metalevel information about a particular slot in a unit. For example we might want to indicate that the population of a state is likely to change slowly even though we don't know the rate at which it changes. So that we would have

```
Pennsylvania
  capital: (Harrisburg)
 *population: (18,000,000)
  stateOf: (UnitedStatesOfAmerica)
  majorCities: (Philadelphia Pittsburgh Scranton)

SeeUnitFor-population.Pennsylvania
  instanceOf: (SeeUnit)
  modifiesUnit:(Pennsylvania)
  modifiesSlot:(population)
         *rateofchange: ()

SeeUnitFor-rateofchange.SeeUnitFor-Population.Pennsylvania
  instanceOf; (SeeUnit)
  modifiesUnit: (SeeUnitFor-population.Pennsylvania)
  modifiesSlot: (rateofchange)
  qualitativeValue: (low)
```

SlotEntryDetails are similar to SeeUnits except that rather than referring to the whole of a slot they refer to only one value. Tuhs by starring the member Philadelphia in the majorCities slot we could add more detail on that city – although it is likely that there would be a unit for Philadelphia itself. By creating

SeeUnitfor-Philadelphia ε majorCities.Pennsylvania

one is able to add information about Philadelphia that is specific to the fact that it is a major city of Pennsylvania.

In addition to storing a value for each slot, CycL maintains other information about every slot of every unit. Specifically

- A truth value for each entry in the value,

- A symbolic justification for why that entry is present in the value

- Bookkeeping information used by the truth maintenance facility

- Some of the properties that each entry inherits just by being in the slot

- Information pertaining to the attitudes of agents towards this proposition.

As we saw earlier when we discussed frame based representations there are certain things that are difficult to represent in the frame based paradigm. Typical examples are

- Disjunctions (Jim's hair is red or his eyes are blue)

- Quantified Statements (Some politicians take bribes)

- Relationships between slot values (People are younger than their parents)

- Negations (Fred doesn't play tennis)

Although it would have been posible to introduce special units that would allow one to make each of these statements it seems easier to introduce a *constraint language* that can be used directly for making these statements. If one wants to make constraints and frames "look" the same one can think of a predicate such as the above as being represented by a unit.

The constraint mechanism is coupled with the inheritance mechanism of the frames. Constraints are inherited along various of the arcs that are used are found in the inheritedSlotConstraints slot of many of the units lower down the hierarchy.

6.2.3 Inference in Cyc

Most intelligent systems conventionally use just one inferencing system geared to the representation and language used. Cyc however introduces the idea of an *inference template*. The process of adding new information to the knowledge base requires that the system have a substantial facility for truth maintenance. What has been done in Cyc is that a number of standard kinds of rules of inference have been identified and a streamlined way of running each of them provided. Broadly therefor we can divide the inferencing system in Cyc into two parts.

- Inference based upon the inference templates. This is managed automatically by the system.

- Inference based upon an **agenda**. This can be controlled by the user.

A review of all the inference templates would take us beyond the scope of this book. We will however discuss some of them in order to give the flavour. The interested reader is referred to section 3.3 of [66].

Inference by following links: As a frame based system it is natural to provide for inference methods that follow the links in the system. Some of these are as follows:

- **Inverses** Often it is the case that for a specific relation $P(x, y)$ it does not matter from the point of view of semantics whether we assert $P(x, y)$ or its inverse $P'(y, x)$. Thus $parent(x, y)$ and $child(y, x)$ have exactly the same meaning. Cyc should therefor update both a relation and its inverse whenever this kind of relationship holds. In fact Cyc goes further; if a new slot is created Cyc tries to create an inverse slot for it.

- **Genl Slots** For certains slots s of a unit u it will be the case that all the values will be a subset of the values in another slot. Thus there is an entry $s.GenlSlots$ indicating that this relationship holds.

- **Transfer Through** Used to handle inferences of the form "a person usually has the same last name as his sons". A slot $s.transfersThrough$ is provided for this kind of information. (Like any frame based system this rule can be overridden at a more specific level). The form of rule that is covered by this can be written

$$\forall x, y, z \ s(x, y) \wedge s'(x, z) \rightarrow s(x, y)$$

- **Inheritance** This is used for carrying values along chains of a given length.

- **toCompute** Used when one slot is defined in (computational) terms of other slots. Slots whose value is found this way have a *toCompute* slot. It should be noted that this is used for computation not as a constraint, you cannot have a collection of slots each of which is defined using a toCompute in terms of the others.

- **Constraints On Slots** Various slots can be provided that do represent constraints on the values that can appear in a given slot.

- **Daemons** Functions that are to be run whenever a slot value changes. Since this is a form of side effect its use should be limited.

In addition there are a number of templates for plausible inference. These are akin to *transfers.through*. These allow Cyc to "guess" values for slots.

Each of these inference templates has a different cost associated with it. Because of this there are several versions of the *get* function that retrieves slot values. The numbers attached to them have purely historical significance.

get0 Just access the data structure.

get4 Try some of the simpler, faster rules such as toCompute, genl-Slots.

get6 Try the above and some more complicated rules such as Slot constraints and full backward inheritance.

get8 Try even the "guessing" mechanisms.

The choice of level of *get* to use is determined by the user, based upon the task requirements. By contrast there is only one level of the *put* function, since the need to keep the knowledge base consistent requires that constraints, inverses and so on must be updated.

This choice of different levels for the retrieval function is the way in which Cyc deals with "deep" versus "shallow" knowledge. All the knowledge is available to the system and each reasoning template has a different depth allowing the user explicit control over how "deep" the knowledge that is used should be. It is assumed that the "shallow" knowledge is more readily retrievable.

6.2.4   Large Scale Control in Cyc

Large scale control in Cyc is provided in two ways, by the use of an *agenda* and by the use of *structures and scripts*. In truth these mechanisms are not quite of the same character but I have chosen to treat them together because they work at a coarser level than the inference mechanisms described in the previous section. Most obviously they are not built into the system in the way that the inference templates are and therefor they are more subject to control by the user.

The Agenda

The agenda is nothing more than a priority queue of tasks. Control is exerted by having the system loop finding the first task that matches a set of given conditions and then executing it.

A *task* is a script, which is to say that it is an instance of Script but it must in fact also be an specialization (spec) to SolvingAProblem. Every task must have a slot howToRunTask. This is a lisp function of one argument (the argument effectively being the task itself). In the case that the function actually executes the task the task is called primitive. In the case that it is not primitive there are a number of default interpreters that fill the slot howToRunTask. The most general of these is the *default executrix*, this performs as follows:

1. Check to see if the task is primitive. Also check to see if there are circumstances which indicate that the primitive solution (which might be brute force) should not be invoked.

2. If the task does not have subtasks and the executrix has never tried to find subtasks for it try to do so.

   (a) If there is a special means of finding subtasks, use it else

(b) If X.structure exists, instantiate it, else

(c) Call (*Get6* #*%subTasks*). If this returns NIL, then

(d) Create a new task X' that will try to find subtasks for X and put it on the agenda.

3. If no subtasks are found and there is no lisp function to use exit with failure

4. If there are subtasks and X is being executed again – this means that the results of the subtasks must now be combined

   (a) There may be an X.howToCombineSubtasks slot

   (b) Some other Cyc inference mechanism may exist to combine the tasks

   If this step is successful the executrix exits having filled the slot X.taskStatus.TaskComplete.

5. Getting to this point more or less means that you have failed. The executrix will pass over the task (give up) and hope for the best.

The above description has a few loose ends. I have not described how the next task is selected nor have I said exactly what a script or structure is. I turn to this now. In order for a task X to be chosen it must be both executable and be such that there is no executable task Y that is preferred to X.

For a task to be executable it must satisfy

- The task is not yet complete as indicated by X.TaskStatus

- There is no reason not to run the task – there is a predicate X.taskNonExecutabilityPredicate that is consulted for this.

- There is some reason to run the task – there is a predicate X.taskExecutabilityPredicate that is consulted for this.

A task X is *preferred* to a task Y when either

- Y.morePreferredTasks.X or

- Neither X nor Y is listed on the other's morePreferredTasks slot and X.taskPriority is greater than Y.taskPriority.

Scripts and Structures

Scripts are the basic units of Cyc that are used to describe the changes that occur when an event takes place. There are two fundamental classes of scripts which partition the unit SomethingOccurring

- Tangible objects being subjected to physical forces

- Intelligent agents making decisions.

Scripts contain constraints

- Typing the actors – eating must have an animal as its performer,

- *Intra*actor constraints – usually eating is preceeded by hunger

- *Inter*actor constraints – eating involves contact between eater and eatee.

Scripts thus represent the structure of events. It is assumed that all relevant changes will be listed in the script. This deals with the frame problem.

Structures describe the basic constraints that hold between the constituent parts of an object. As such they are similar to scripts except that they relate more to static objects whereas scripts are used for dynamic objects.

6.2.5　　Some other aspects of Cyc

There are a number of other aspects of Cyc that are worth commenting on. I have gathered them together here.

Reasoning about an agent's beliefs

There are a number of occasions when an intelligent system needs to be able to reason about the beliefs and motivations of another agent. Natural language provides a good example of this. We will often ask a question which is not literally the one we want answered, as for example when we phone someone and ask

Is Fred there?

What we really want to do is talk to Fred. Similarly if Fred and Bert have the same phone number and I know Bert's phone number, do I know Fred's phone number (or rather do I know that I know it?!)

The approach that Cyc eventually takes to this problem is to view the knowledge base as organized into a collection of several knowledge bases each tied to the agent who believes them. The set of facts believed by the agent A is denoted $KB(A)$. A more general notion regarding the beliefs that A has about B's beliefs is denoted by $KB(A, B)$ (with similar definitions for $KB(A, B, C, \ldots)$.)

Normally reasoning about an individual's beliefs takes place within a knowledge base $KB(A, B)$. However there are occasions where an agent A may be justified in *projecting* his beliefs onto another. That is in adding a fact F from $KB(A)$ to $KB(A, B)$. It should be noted that if $PRED$ is the condition that allows one to do this then $PRED$ is a function of the unit, slot, and value that give the fact, and of the agent B, but $PRED$ is evaluated in $KB(A)$.

The mechanism can be used to support "what-if" reasoning by creating a temporary agent who believes the assumption.

Cyc's Ontology: The Highest Level of Control

Much of the structuring of Cyc has to do with the choice of what things get to be units. Rather than reproduce the outline of the hierarchy that appears in [66] I will restrict myself to a number of comments that I believe characterize the way in which the selection was made.

Individual objects should be grouped into categories since this provides a convenient way to make inferences about similar objects. Appropriate slots are

- Default properties of most members of the category,

- Recognition rules for members of the category,

- Special heuristics for dealing with a member of the category,

- Questions that can be meaningfully asked about members of the category,

- How many members are there in the category.

This last point is somewhat important because it emphasizes that one should only make a category when it is interesting in some way. Often this means that there are several members of the category. (Although the category of odd perfect numbers is interesting if only because its size is unknown.) Another guide for the reasonableness of a particular category is that it should at least have a slot canHaveSlots which indicates that the category does capture something interesting. Finally we note that we can create a category when some of the things that can be said about the category cannot equally well said about some larger category.

Analogy in Cyc

One of the things that Cyc is intended to be able to do is find analogies. Unfortunately as we have seen earlier analogy is not an easy subject to get hold of in the AI context. The intended attack on this problem in Cyc will be to use divide and conquer to break down phenomena into subtypes and handle each one separately: building upon a large (millions) pool of objects substances, events, sets, ideas, etc., which can be targets of analogy. As yet the system is not large enough for it to have had a chance to make any analogies.

Retrospect on Cyc

What can one say about a system as large and ambitious as Cyc? Perhaps this is best done by contrasting it with Soar. The most obvious difference between the two lies in the fact that Soar is basically a top down system that acquires its own methods from the chunking mechanism, whereas Cyc is much more of a bottom up system whose problem solving system is much less well defined. Both systems seek to capture several inference methods in one system, Soar through the universal weak method and Cyc through its system of special encodings of inference methods.

Cyc as it stands at present is more of a respository of Knowledge than an intelligent agent. It is capable of maintaining internal consistency. For the moment it does not seem that the problem solving skills have been fully incorporated into it. In this sense it is complementary to Soar. Perhaps when it is large enough to find analogies it will be able to learn in new ways. The target date for this kind of result is 1994.

6.3 Blackboards

One of the aspects of problem solving is that there are often many different sources of knowledge that must be used when working on a particular problem. Scene analysis provides a particularly apposite model. In trying to interpret a picture intelligent systems can be expected to rely upon information derived from color, shading, pattern, and from the expectations that the agent has at the time that the scene is being viewed. Perhaps the most successful model that addresses the problem of integrating information from diverse sources is the *blackboard model* [75].

The origins of the blackboard model can be found in Selfridge's *pandemonium* model [87]: here a set of independent demons shouts out its evaluation in proportion to they way in which what the see fits their nature. As we shall see the blackboard model resembles also a kind of "principled" neural network. The knowledge sources correspond to more sophisticated neurons, indeed some knowledge sources within a blackboard system could be based upon neural nets. The first blackboard systems were used in the HEARSAY system for speech recognition and in HASP which was used for interpreting data from various sources for ship detection. Details of these and other applications can be found in the articles by Penny Nii [75], [76].

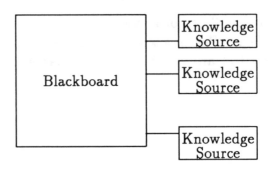

Figure 6.1: The Blackboard Model

6.3.1   The Blackboard Model

Figure 6.1 illustrates the major components of the blackboard architecture. These consist of:

The Knowledge Sources. These are *separate* sources of knowledge that will be used to solve the problem.

The Blackboard Data Structure. The problem solving state data are kept in a *global* database. This provides the only mechanism through which the knowledge sources are able to interact.

Control. The blackboard architecture does not specify a particular model of control, rather the knowledge sources themselves react opportunistically to changes in the blackboard.

This description is a very high level view of the blackboard model and does not begin to describe that way in which the various knowledge sources can in fact interact through the use of the blackboard. In what follows we will take this up in more detail.

Before doing this however it is worth pointing out that to date most blackboard models actually include some form of monitor process. This is not in fact a necessary part of the model rather it is a consequence of the fact that the model has been implemented on sequential machines, forcing some serialization of the access to the blackboard. Partially for this reason some have advocated that control be lodged in the blackboard itself [48]. It seems likely that with the development of parallel languages blackboard systems which are truly opportunistic in their implementation.

6.3.2 The Blackboard Framework

It is convenient to think of blackboard systems as assembling the solution by building partial solutions and patching them together. The precise nature of the architecture will depend on the application in question but there are a number of general principles that seem to hold across the spectrum of blackboard systems.

In general the blackboard itself consists of several 'layers' corresponding to a hierarchical decomposition of the problem. Indeed if there is more than one way to obtain a hierarchical decomposition of the problem the blackboard can have more than one panel, each panel corresponding to a different decomposition.

In describing the detailed structure of a blackboard system it is best to have a particular application in mind. For the purpose of the explanation that I will give I have chosen to use scene understanding as an example. An appropriate hierarchy structure for the blackboard will then be

Highest	Category of Object	House, Road, Field, etc..
	Object	
Lowest	Characteristic Region	High Contrast, Color, etc.

The knowledge Sources each contribute information that will lead to a solution of the problem. It must take its current information from the blackboard and update it using its specialized knowledge. A knowledge source can be represented as a procedure, a set of rules or logic assertions, the choice depends on the nature of the knowledge source. Only knowledge sources are capable of modifying the blackboard. Each knowledge source determines the conditions under which it can modify the blackboard, in particular there are *preconditions* that must be satisfied before the body of a knowledge source is activated.

The blackboard holds the computational and solution state data needed by, and produced by, the knowledge sources. The objects in the blackboard consist of objects from the solution space. They can be input data, partial solutions, alternatives and final solutions. As we saw above the blackboard is hierarchically organized into levels. Information on a given level serves as input to a knowledge source which in turn creates input either for the same or other levels. Thus a knowledge source that has identified an object as a road can prevent another knowledge source form recognizing the same object as bare soil.

Although the knowledge sources are supposed to respond opportunistically to changes in the blackboard there is a set of *control modules* that monitor the state of the blackboard and decide what action to take next. In particular they serve to establish the *focus of attention*, which is the next thing to be processed. The overall pattern of problem solving activity is as follows:

1. A knowledge source makes changes to object(s) on the blackboard. Records of these changes are kept in a global data structure that holds control information.

2. Each knowledge source indicates the contribution that it can make to the new solution state.

3. The control module sets the focus of attention.

4. Depending on the information in the focus of attention a control module prepares it for execution as follows:

   (a) If the focus of attention is a knowledge source then a set of blackboard objects is chosen to serve as the context of its invocation.

   (b) If the focus of attention is a blackboard object, then a knowledge source is chosen to which will process that object. This is an event scheduling approach.

   (c) If the focus of attention is a knowledge source and a blackboard object, then the knowledge source is ready for execution. The source is executed with the context.

Finally criteria must be provided to determine when the problem-solving process is to be terminated. Usually one of the knowledge sources will provide this. Termination means either that the problem is solved or the system is unable to determine a solution.

Ther are a number of special aspects of the blackboard model that are worth pointing out.

The hierarchical structure of the blackboard permits reasoning that allows for interaction between high and low level information We have already seen that in our example on scene recognition the identification of a region as being of one type inhibits its recognition as being of another type, but the idea can be carried further. For example a control module could "hypothesize" that a given region is a house and "focus the attention" of the system on verifiying or disproving the hypothesis. (The jig-saw puzzle analogy is apposite here. One finds a piece that one would like to place and based upon its colour guesses that it is part of a house, leading to an attempt to join it to other pieces known to be parts of houses.)

Even if a blackboard system fails to solve a problem it is likely to have accumulated a number of partial solutions. For real-time systems where even a partial solution may be of value these can be used to determine the action to be taken by an autonomous system.

Control information can be built into the blackboard itself, this is the approach advocated by B. Hayes-Roth in [48]. In effect this only requires that control information be posted on an appropriate panel of the blackboard. The control modules described above are themselves only a form of knowledge source whose expertise happens to be in the area of control. Conflicts between different control principles can be resolved by a conflict resolution module.

6.4 Hypertext as a Knowledge Base

The design of the interface to an intelligent system is not really one of the topics that I have chosen to address in this book. However I do feel that is is appropriate to make some remarks on the subject, particularly since the emergence of hypertext has provided us with an interface system that matches some of the knowledge representation methods that have been successful.

In constructing an intelligent system, particularly a large one, it is necessary to provide the knowledge engineer with a way to keep track of the structure and data in the knowledge base. To some extent one can hope that automatic internal mechanisms will be effective in detecting such things as contradictory data and other inconsistencies. However the ability to view the knowledge base at various granularities is highly desirable. Hypertext seems to provide a natural way of building the kind of interface that will be needed.

This natural fit can be seen best in frame based systems. Each frame sits in a hierarchy so that one can move through the knowledge base by following the links between frames. Lenat is quite explicit the the editor used to enter new knowledge into Cyc is based upon hypertext ideas. This fit is a consequence of the network model that underlies hypertext. A weakness at the present (although some would call this a strength) is that hypertext links can join objects of diferent types. Unless one take the view that the objects in hypertext are just blocks of text and that the links join a key 'phrase' to another text block.

In the case of a system that has been built upon one of the knowledge representation paradigms that we have discussed here this latter problem does not matter too much since the system structure provides a logic for the hypertext system to emulate. In any case I expect that hypertext (and hypermedia) will become the paradigm for constructing the user interface to intelligent systems. Particularly as these systems are designed for use by persons whose primary intention is to apply them rather than use them as research tools.

One final point about hypertext. At present hypertext knowledge bases occupy a role in knowledge representation akin to that occupied some years ago by the network model of databases. That is to say before the emergence of the relational model. While netweork methods are still used to implement relational databases the interface is based upon the relational model. We do not yet have the kind of uniform view of knowledge that we do of data, when we do, we can expect the interface paradigm to change again, although hypertext methods may well give us the efficiency we will need.

6.5   Review of Large Systems

In reviewing the large systems that we have looked at I will be interested in the degree to which the structure of the systems determines the language used to talk about them. Interestingly enough two of

System	Soar	Cyc	Blackboards
KR	Augmentation	Frames	KS
Inference	Rule Based	Special Rules	KS Dependant

Table 6.1: Comparison of Inference Methods

the systems (Cyc and Soar) are written in LISP (although Soar was originally written in OPS5), this seems more to be a matter of the general preference for LISP amongst workers in the field in the USA.

The following table gives the dominant influences on the structure of the systems. For this purpose blackboard systems are treated as a single type although there can be variations from system to system.

In Soar the central choice was that the system should be impasse driven and should use subgoaling as its "universal" problem solving mechanism. The choice of a rule based system as the language in which to write the system provides the other major influence on the structure of Soar. Note that the subgoaling mechanism favours the choice of the stack architecture within the system. Although the choice of productions as the language of the system appears to have been one of the earliest apects of the design it is a logical choice to go with the impasse system because it is possible to classify the impasses and then prescribe what is to be done in each case.

In Cyc the central choice appears to have been that of using the frame as the basic unit for knowledge representation. The special inference mechanisms are optimized in a way that accords well with the frame structure by providing special links (such as inverse) that speed up consistency checks and retrievals. We saw that it is however necessary to provide an additional constraint language for those constraints that do not fall well into the frame based system. This is a consequence of what is after all the major design decision about Cyc namely that it should have an encyclopedic collection of "common sense" knowledge. Frames serve well to represent the structure of both complex objects and events so that tasks and processes can be decomposed. In this context the use of an agenda for high level control seems to arise quite naturally since the decomposition of a structure leaves undetermined the order in which parts of the structure are to be investigated.

From the perspective of the other systems a blackboard system seems to have much less structure because of its opportunistic nature. The basic model of co-operating knowledge sources that contribute opportunistically to the solution of a problem is however just as valid as the two previous systems. It does indeed permit a greater degree of flexibility in the way in which knowledge can be represented within a given system. However there will remain a problem of translating the knowledge between a given knowledge source and the blackboard. One place where this is particularly relevant is in the translation of uncertainty between different systems. The opportunistic nature of the control does permit blackboard systems to design in real time considerations in a way that is less easy to do in the other two systems.

Chapter 7

Representation, Reason, Language

In this chapter I will bring together the work of the earlier chapters, in an attempt to present a unified view of the place of language, representation and reasoning in AI.

There are a number of general issues that I will discuss in this summary chapter. In some sense they are a review of the material that has been discussed earlier. Only this time I hope that it will be possible to see how they fit into the general framework of Representation, Reason and Language in AI. The topics that I have chosen to emphasize are representation, inference, and control. There is no specific section on language since this is an integral part of the discussion of each of the other topics.

In the body of the book I have used both concrete examples and abstract formulations of the topics under discussion. It seems to me important to understand that these are both part of the whole enterprise. A sound theoretical understanding of the limitations of a model is necessary if one is to build systems that are reliable. Indeed one of the main difficulties inherent in the Artificial Intelligence field is the fact that our models are still nowhere near strong enough to allow us to argue convincingly about anything other than comparitively small systems. However as we have seen even large systems are assembled from smaller parts and according to principled construction methods that should eventually allow us to make realistic assertions about

197

their capabilities.

7.1 Representation

Knowledge representation will continue to play a central role in the construction of any intelligent system. The examples that we have examined show that the choice of representation is perhaps the most influential single aspect of the system.

Intelligent systems must be able to represent complex systems. They must therefor be able to find ways of structuring their knowledge about such systems. To the extent that one wishes a system to be "universal" it is desirable that

- The system have available to it a rich set of structuring mechanisms, so that by indentifying the structure the method of handling it can be easily retrieved;

- The system have a small enough number of structuring mechanisms so that the correct one can be found as quickly as possible.

As is usually the case with desirable characteristics one is pulled in two opposing directions. Examination of the systems described in chapter 6 shows that this can be approached in three ways. Soar elects to use essentially just one mechanism, that of the hierarchy, through subgoaling. The blackboard architecture is willing (at least conceptually) to provide a knowledge source for every way in which a problem can be decomposed. Cyc appears to be willing to adopt a compromise position, a problem may have many structures but only a few will be represented, leaving the analogy mechanism to find others.

In this regard human intelligence probably adopts the solution favoured by the blackboard systems. We seem to remember the structures that we need most. When our "weak methods" fail we find someone whose expertise contains a "strong model" of the process. Distributed models of intelligence also support this view of the decomposition problem.

7.1.1 Decomposition

In fact hierarchical decomposition can be described as the "universal weak method of decomposition" in that it can be adapted to most questions that intelligent systems will have to face. The way in which the decomposition gets done depends very much on the representation. Consider the following examples

- Diagnostic problems. If the reasoning is goal directed then the problem decomposes into considering each possible diagnosis in turn.

- Logical Representation, in the case where the goal is described as a conjunction it is usual to decompose it into the successive acquisition of the terms of the conjunction. The fool's disk example shows though that the precise specification of an equivalent conjunction may make the problem solvable.

- Representation by a machine suggests decomposition into a cascade of machines, using powerful algebraic analogies.

- Graphical representation usually suggests that some kind of search should be done.

There is another trade-off that must be made when representations are chosen. On the one hand the generic hierarchical decomposition has the virtue of wide applicability, but this very versatility means that the mechanism for assembling the pieces, which must also be fairly general, will not necessarily give a particularly efficient way of solving the problem. On the other hand choice of a highly structured decomposition gives one a better chance of finding efficient solutions. Furthermore the more structure that one builds into a problem the more likely one is to be to solve it once a match has been found.

Fortunately the notions of a hierarchy can be used to help resolve this difficulty. One can impose a hierarchical structure on the structures themselves. Problems (used here in a wider sense than the usual one, I intend any kind of difficulty that may face an intelligent system) should be classified in a way that allows one to retrieve as quickly as possible the method that applies to them. The ontology used in

Cyc, and indeed the whole structure of an object oriented language is directed towards solving this most basic problem of intelligence.

We can list some of the requirements of a representation scheme as follows:

- It should permit sufficient internal organization so that the type of the object (problem) being represented can be easily classified.

- It should be flexible enough so that decompositions of problems can be expressed naturally in terms of the representation

- It should use as few special structures as possible

We should elaborate on the last point since it is in some sense the most important. Success in the computational and inferential marketplace seems to have gone (except where powerful players have distorted the reward structure) to those languages that have used a few simple ideas. This is not to say that the resulting language will be simple, rather it argues that the choice of the right small number of building blocks seems to be the critical issue.

How does this affect the representation problems that we have listed above? We have seen that the critical issues seems to be retrieval and flexibility (this latter is sometimes called expressivity). If we address retrieval first we need to take into account the polymorphic nature of most problems in intelligence. The standard techniques of AI, such as search, apply to very different problems. In fact one (albeit still poorly understood) technique namely analogy, depends on the possibility of being able to match objects of different types. This argues that the language of an intelligent system should be as close to being type independant as is "safe". Objects should understand just enough of their nature so that "obvious" type errors are not made. In practice this has meant that AI languages have been type free as in LISP or Prolog, but the examples of Smalltalk and ML show that this is not necessary.

Furthermore it is necessary to build retrieval structures where the objects that are to be retrieved can be of different types and are often retrieved by a mechanism that is intended to mimic the associative nature of human memory. The characteristic retrieval method in AI is pattern matching. By basing their data representation on the list LISP and prolog are able to build pattern matchers that incorporate the tree structuring possibilities of lists.

It is important to remark that at this point I am not making any claim that the use of lists and pattern matching as done in LISP or Prolog is "best". Indeed from the point of view of efficiency it is likely to be a poor choice. On the other hand the process of constructing the system is made easier because of the way in which these languages manipulate lists so easily. (For a C programmer the use of pointers and the ability to cast types will allow him to produce similar facilities in a C program. This involves much playing "fast and loose" with the typing that software engineering practice would condemn.)

7.1.2 Some Specific Representation problems

In this subsection I want to discuss some specific representation problems that I have not managed to address earlier.

Arity of relations.

One of the most successful uniform models for data is the relation, conventionally represented as a table. Amongst relations the binary relation is particularly well understood. Relations in a world model can be used to represent both objects with their attributes as in

person(name:john, hair:brown, eyes:blue, height:180cm)

and processes as in

loves(john, mary)

there is however a subtle distinction in that an object may have many attributes whereas a process (in the sense used here) tends to be represented by a relation whose arity is relatively small. (Some of this discussion is adapted from [66]and [38]).

A relation can be considered to be a predicate, where the tuples that belong to the relation are just those for which the predicate is true. Binary predicates (or relations) have the distinct advantage that they are more easily treated in a formal way than predicates of higher arity. In particular every binary relation R on a set $X \times Y$ gives rise to an inverse relation R^{-1} on $Y \times X$. This means that binary relations can be used for navigation through a knowledge base, where they can be represented by links between sets. Relations of higher arity do not have quite this nice representational interpretation.

Besides this representational convenience of low arity predicates there is a further bias in their favour that comes from the structure of natural language. When simple sentences are interpreted in terms of relations it is hard to find verbs that have arities that exceed three. Most direct statements are of arity two

> John loves Mary.
>
> Mary saw a bear.

There are many cases where the arity is three.

> John threw the dog a stick.
>
> Mary writes a letter to John.

A few of arity four:

> John bet Mary five pounds that he would win.
>
> Fred lent Henry the money for the ticket.

It is interesting that the examples of arity four verbs (bet, buy, lend) all seem to relate to formal transactions. This accords with the idea that higher arity relations are more "artificial" than the more "natural" lower arity ones. Indeed most of the examples of higher arity relations seem to deal with "constructed" objects.

> polygon(A,B,C,D,E,F).
>
> route(London, Paris, Geneva, Turin, Venice, Vienna)

Thus it seems that it is realistic to assume that it is only necessary to provide special mechanisms for dealing with ternary and quaternary relations. Note for example that by allowing lists as elements in a relation the arity of the route relation can be reduced.

> route(London, Vienna,
> [London, Paris, Geneva, Turin, Venice, Vienna]).

Retrieval By Value

One of the greatest challenges in constructing a knowledge base is the mastering the retrieval problem. Natural intelligence has managed to devise an extremely effective associative memory. For artificially intelligent systems the problem is still largely unresolved. As we move towards real time intelligent systems it will become progressively more critical to resolve this problem.

One way in which this can be done is by the incorporation of special purpose mechanisms. For example in Cyc the inverse links allow one to move in both directions along most links. In some implementations of prolog it is possible to index facts on one or more of the fields in the relation.

An important aspect of this retrieval problem is the linearity of most representation schemes. In principle the user of a system should not be required to know the order in which the fields in a relation are stored, and yet it is often the case that such knowledge is either explicitly required of the user, or if it is not required there may be advantages if one happens to know it. For example to refer back to the prolog indexing, this is usually restricted to the leading fields, with the consequence that other mechanisms need to be used for retrieval on later fields.

It is here that the distinction between prototype and product becomes important. In a prototype one can use a language or system in which retrieval may be slow, but the language matches the structure of the system. In the product one can use special retrieval mechanisms that may require a different structure internally, while implementing the original solution.

7.2 Inference

In our previous discussion of reasoning we divided the inference mechanisms into two classes

- Logical Inference

- Graphical Inference

Logical inference uses the conventional forms of a theorem prover, whereas graphical inference works by representing the problem to be solved in terms of finding a path through some graph. We can see how each of the systems that we have discussed use graphical inference to replace specific modes of logical inference so that they become built into the system. Since Cyc is most explicit about this we begin with it.

Compiling Inference in Cyc. We saw that Cyc has a large number of specific inference methods compiled into it. It is worth illustrating how one of these replaces a logical argument with a specific link. The most obvious example where this is used is in the case of inverses. In logical terms the inference in question is

If s and s' are inverse relations then

$$\forall x, y. \ s(x,y) \leftrightarrow s'(y,x)$$

In Cyc this becomes

Place s' as the sole entry on s.inverse.

The other compiled inferences are treated similarly. That is say rules of logical inference are replaced by slot values. So that logical inference is replaced by link following. Put in other words, logical inference is built into the structure of the network of frames that comprise the knowledge base.

Compiling Inference in ALICE. Without wishing to repeat all the details of Laurière's system, it will be recalled that the constraints are as far as possible translated into explicit reductions of the graph which represents the possible solution. Those constraints that cannot be so reduced are dealt with by explicit search. Once again we see that the specific choice of representation determines the language that can be used for constraint satisfaction.

Compiling Inference in Soar. Elements in working memory in Soar are given by augmentations of objects. These an be thought of as attribute-value lists attached to each object. The inference methods in Soar (which it should be recalled is a problem solving system and uses search as its primary mechanism) rely upon the Soar rules for resolving impasses together with special rules that depend on the problem of interest. The augmentations of the objects allow the focus of the system to switch to any context which is linked to the current one. So here again inference is compiled into links in the knowledge base. The method is one step removed from that of Cyc since there will have to be a rule that adds the augmentation to the object and thus creates the link.

Compiling Inference in a Blackboard. Since the blackboard model is more flexible than the other systems it is less straightforward to claim that specific inference methods are compiled into the blackboard model. However the potential for doing just this is very much present. Any knowledge source can be considered as a compiled inference method. This permits one to optimize each knowledge source independently.

Thus each intelligent system that we have examined uses the way in which it represents knowledge to allow it to incorporate certain kinds of compiled inference so that it will not have to search when it needs to make this kind of inference.

However there are still problems that remain in this area. As one adds more and more links to a frame based system to account for special inference techniques the knowledge base gets larger with a concomitant degradation of performance. To some extent one can hope that machines will get larger and faster rapidly enough so that this can be discounted, nevertheless it seems to me important that we find ways to limit the proliferation of links. To this end we need to be able to determine which methods of inference are likely to be effective in a given situation. To some extent Soar does this through its learning mechanism. Indeed this it would seem is the critical value of learning as a mechanism for compiling knowledge, because it means that the knowledge that does get compiled is exactly that which is required for the situation.

An interesting idea in this context is the use of "teaching" mechanisms. This is not an area that I have discussed earlier and I wish only to make a brief comment here. We have all had an experience where we have been doing something in a particular way for some time and then someone shows us another "easier" way which we then adopt. How can one model this with a computer system? Since this is one of the most effective ways in which we can improve performance, it would seem desirable to be able to do this for machine systems.

7.3   Control

In considering control in intelligent systems we have seen that one of the central issues is that of "focus" and it is on this aspect that we will concentrate.

There is a sense in which every data structure has associated to it a natural control structure. Furthermore this is often then reflected in languages that use a particular data structure. The obvious examples are the array and the list. Arrays correspond naturally to determinate loops and lists to recursive processes and indeterminate loops. I want to discuss the extent to which a similar phenomenon occurs with a knowledge base. That is to what extent does the choice of knowledge representation determine the way in which control is handled in a system.

When we consider the systems that are closely based upon a specific language, such as for example a prolog based system, then it is clear that it will be natural to use backward chaining to control the inference, since this is the natural mechanism for prolog. Furthermore iteration of any kind must be achieved through recursion. If other control structures are required then one must either build a meta-interpreter in prolog that implements the desired control, or use an agenda that will replace the depth-first search natural to prolog. While neither of these things are necessarily difficult they do impair the efficiency of the system.

On the other hand this ability to provide custom built meta-interpreters and agendas means that a prolog based system can be designed in such a way that the control mechanism is an explicit separate part of the system. Of course this is not a peculiarity of prolog, this kind of separation could be achieved with any language.

Returning to the issue of the way in which the structure of the knowledge base influences control we can consider the case of production systems. Considered as $<condition, action>$ pairs productions are nothing other than control rules. So that a production system from this viewpoint is built from control rules. In fact as the example of Soar shows there is much more to it than this. At any given point in the progress of the system it is likely that the *condition* part of several rules will fire setting up the possibility of a number of different actions. Therefore production systems must have *conflict resolving* rules for deciding upon which action to take. It is these rules that will largely determine the behaviour of the system. There seem to be a number of general principles that apply which we can disengage from the examples of the large systems such as Cyc and Soar.

- Prefer compiled knowledge over "deep" knowledge, (if the compiled knowledge fails you can always come back to the deep knowledge.)

- When making a choice prefer the option that will yield the most information if it is successful.

- Other things being equal make the choice that least limits ones subsequent choices.

- Build in some way of remembering successful choices, at a suitably general level.

These principles are not in themselves enough to completely determine the choice of rule to use in case of a conflict but they do provide strong guidance as to the correct choice. Notice once again how the system allows one to explicitly localize control information into an identifiable subset of the system.

Semantic networks provide a different view of control, particularly as it affects the question of focus. In the systems we described above focus is determined by the control rules some of which may put things on an agenda or take them off. On the other hand in a semantic network each object is responsible for activating its neigbours through the linking mechanism. The following example shows how this might work.

We can consider a a system designed to understand simple stories that is built somewhat in the manner of Cyc using a frame based system. Such a system could have an UnderstandStory Frame which would be a script whose most important responsibility would be the location of the correct script for understanding the story. Assuming that the correct frame is identified a link to it would be established and traversed. At this point control is passed to the frame for the particular story, BankHoldUp say.

The frame BankHoldUp will be a script that describes the structure of a bank hold up. Thus it is entirely responsible for the control of the process at this level. It may itself be linked to further scripts, CarChase for example, which will themselves be responsible for a further level of control.

Thus in this kind of structure we have a very different view of control than the one that went with the production system model. Control is now localized with each process. Although overall control will still reside in the top level frame. This kind of model is appropriate for distributed systems where the local resources are more likely to dictate the rate of progress than the originating central system.

The blackboard model takes a somewhat different view of the control process. Indeed it is specific that interaction with the blackboard is to be opportunistic. In fact we saw that there is necessarily a process whose responsibility it is to decide which of several competing knowledge sources will be allowed to modify the blackboard. This is of course a logical consequence of the fact that the blackboard is a shared resource with all the resulting restrictions on access. Something has to be charged with resolving the "readers-writers" problem.

Nevertheless the blackboard itself can incorporate a measure of control data. That is to say it can be architected in such a way that the blackboard itself chooses who is able to modify it at a given point in time. Indeed this will even permit a level of granularity that will allow several knowledge sources to apparently access the blackboard simultaneously if their actions do not interfere with one another.

In addition to the control contained within the blackboard (or scheduler if that is used) there is the question of control within the knowledge sources themselves. This of course depends on the structure of the knowledge base itself. A blackboard architecture thus permits the division of control into

- Central Control determined by the state of the blackboard,

- Local control within each knowledge source

One final issue concerning blackboards is what one might term the "translation" problem. Each knowledge source can have its own internal representation of the problem or part of the problem on which it is working. It is however obliged to be able to "translate" this into a form that will be accessible to the other knowledge sources. It is thus unlikely that one can construct a blackboard system by "throwing together" a number of independent knowledge sources. Consideration of the different methods of reasoning under uncertainty will show that different systems can have radically different ways of interpreting their confidence in a given conclusion. The blackboard thus plays an important role in reconciling these differing representation. Indeed it is probably for this reason that blackboard systems rely much more on hypothesize and verify than do other systems. Since the differing hypotheses provide a uniform set of goals towards which the knowledge sources can be directed.

Control in intelligent systems thus falls into one of three groups

1. Central Control

2. Completely localized control

3. Mixed Control, with some central control and some local control.

These correspond, somewhat roughly to the following language models

1. Single thread conventional serial language

2. Parallel thread, parallel processes

3. Time sharing under the control of a central operating system

These linguistic parallels serve as useful models for both design and evaluation of intelligent systems. The parallel model is perhaps the least understood but also the most promising in terms of what we can expect in the near future. The blackboard architecture seems to offer a good compromise for systems that can use some version of hypothesize and test.

7.4   The Closed World

As a final general review topic I would like to discuss a number of questions related to non-monotonicity of certain types of reasoning. One can identify the following problems for the construction of an intelligent agent that impinge on this area.

- Reasoning about the actions of other agents.

- Reasoning with incomplete information,

- Reasoning in a changing environment.

The first of these, reasoning about the actions of other agents, is particularly important for applications involving interactions with humans, such as natural language processing. Typically questions are asked that when interpreted and responded to literally would not have the intended effect. Thus the question

Is James there?

when used by someone beginning a phone call is usually (correctly) interpreted as a request to speak to James, rather than just a question about his location. An intelligent agent would be aware of this.

The accepted way to deal with this problem is to create a model of any agent with whom (which?) the system is to interact. As we saw Cyc makes this quite explicit through the use of knowledge bases that model an agent's beliefs. Note how this method fits into the Cyc methodology in a "seamless" way. It is a quite natural extension of the language of Cyc to cope with the existence of multiple agents.

In fact this process of modeling agents shows quite clearly the way in which the representation reason and language are inevitably tied together. Each agent is represented by a model that carries information about the system's beliefs as to the agents desires, beliefs and plans. Attempts to influence the agent will therefore be based upon this model which will necessarily determine the reasoning process and the language used for this purpose. The ambiguous use of the word language here is in fact quite intentional as it refers both to the internal language used to reason about the agent and to the external language used to "reason with" the agent.

7.4.1   Incomplete Information

Herbert Simon uses the phrase "limited rationality" to describe one of the central problems of intelligence. For the foreseeable future any kind of intelligent agent, human or artificial is bound to have to act without considering all the options in exhaustive detail. However it is not the problem of lack of time to make an exhaustive search that I want to discuss rather it is the problem that there may be important information that is not available to the agent. The process of providing a model for this information is that of a default value imputation. In constructing models that deal with this problem the main difficulty seems to be in providing a mechanism that allows one to eliminate the exceptional cases as quickly as possible. Let us contrast two ways in which this can be done.

In the first way (more or less as it might be done in a semantic network model) if an object does not inherit a default characteristic then the local slot for that value is used to over-ride the inherited one, or a special link is provided indicating that the value is not inherited. This works if the object is well enough defined. However when the object is not well defined as for example in case one knows that one is dealing with a bird but not the type of bird then a second method of the following type can be used.

```
flies(X) :- bird(X), flightless(X), !, fail.
flies(X) :- bird(X).

flightless(emu).
flightless(ostrich).
flightless(kiwi).
```

Obviously this method becomes more cumbersome as the exceptions get larger in number.

Both of these methods however have to contend with the problem that as the agent moves in the world it may discover that an object that was assumed to have the default value for some attribute does not in fact do so. We must therefor structure things so that recovery from this is possible. To this end one needs some mechanism such as that used by Cyc where each attribute has associated to it the justification for its value.

Once again the model that is being used is intimately linked to the reason and language. The model must be flexible enough so that is can represent its own reasoning process so that it can recover it when necessary. Note however that the prolog mechanism described above because it can change its knowledge base will be able (at the price of re-deduction) to accommodate such changes.

7.4.2　Reasoning in a Changing Environment

I have chosen not to discuss real-time systems or systems that reason under changing circumstances. This is not because I consider such systems unimportant. Rather it is because I feel that the language necessary to discuss such systems is not yet adequately developed.

We considered earlier the uestion of representing temporal events and their relationships. What makes this problem different from the other problems that we have looked at is that none of the languages that we have seem to be well adapted to handling time. In large measure this is because the execution of a language is itself an event which is subject to its own time frame.

We are able to model dynamic processes such as the flight of a rocket because the model allows us to compute the orbits faster than they develop in real time. However for many Artificial Intelligence applications we do not have models that can be made to run faster than real time. Indeed sometimes we do not even have the models with any reasonable predictive power. One response to this difficulty is typified by the "naive physics" movement [47]. Typically qualitative arguments are used to replace quantitative ones. Clearly, at some level, this is exactly what humans do. We cannot predict in detail the behaviour of the surface of a liquid in a glass that is being tilted, but we can avoid spilling it. What is necessary is to come up with a model which carries just enough of the important details for one to be able to predict behaviour at the desired level. (It is worth recalling that this is the genesis of the "frame" problem, for if one is to undersatnd how a process evolves it is important to know what remains unchanged.)

Returning to the question of temporally changing environments we se that the critical issues are

- A language that permits one to describe time at the appropriate level of granularity

- Efficient models for determining which attributes of an object are changed by a process and which are unchanged.

These are still areas of active research, both in the Artificial Intelligence community and in the larger computer science community.

7.5 Putting It All Together

The time has come to try and tie all the ideas of this book together and see what they tell us about the enterprise of Artificial Intelligence. Our thesis has been that there is a necessarily intimate relationship between the method of knowledge representation used in a system, the reasoning that the system uses and the language used by the system.

One one level this is a truism, but in fact I believe that the conscious realization of this relationship assists in the construction of systems. We have seen examples of this in our examinations of the ALICE, Cyc and Soar systems so that some of the details should be familiar. What I would like to do now is review the relationship from a more qualitative viewpoint.

One of the more important aspects of the construction of an intelligent system lies in the existence of a two-level nature of any substantial system. The knowledge in the system can be divided between what I have previously referred to as compiled and interpreted knowledge. Compiled knowledge is often heuristic because it is comparable to the learned skills that allow one to do things like ride a bicycle, interpreted knowledge is based upon a deeper model of the subject matter.

Prolog provides a nice example of exactly this distinction. Consider the following knowledge base.

```
grandfather(fred, james).
grandfather(andrew, george).
grandfather(thomas, fred).
```

```
grandfather(X,Z) :- father(X,Y), father(Y,Z).
grandfather(X,Y) :- father(X,Y), mother(Y,Z).

% Data on fatherhood.

% Data on motherhood.
```

The first clauses are examples of compiled knowledge, and the rules are examples of interpreted knowledge. The ordering of the rules in the knowledge base ensures that the system will try the compiled knowledge before the interpreted knowledge. More sophisticated systems will have more levels than just these two. The four levels of the **get** operation in the Cyc system provide one example of this. We can recapitulate the possible levels as follows:

1. Retrieve a value by direct access,

2. Retrieve a value by following a short sequence of links.

3. Retrieve a value by some exhaustive method.

4. Retrieve a value by a "guess".

Direct access to a value should be interpreted as including the use of a calculation from other known values. The use of a short sequence of links corresponds to a partial compilation of knowledge.

There is another division of knowledge representation that is also important and that is the distinction between procedural and declarative knowledge. There is a parallel between procedural knowledge and compiled knowledge in that the information resides in the process used to recover it. Procedural knowledge is in fact the kind of knowledge that learning seeks to obtain. Inevitably declarative knowledge is stored in a way that while it may make verification of a solution straightforward makes the finding of a solution the object of some search procedure. Procedures such as chunking, which are used in Soar, serve to replace the result of a search process with a specific procedure to be followed; that is with explicit compiled knowledge.

A knowledge representation serves to bias the selection of methods for storing compiled knowledge, as well as interpreted knowledge. Network models store compiled knowledge as slots in a frame or in explicit links. Interpreted knowledge lies in the tracing of longer sequences of links and in the provision of explicit control methods. Logical representations can incorporate compiled knowledge by using special purpose predicates. The interpreted knowledge lies in the choice of theorem proving methods.

As a system develops more compiled knowledge the implementation needs change. It becomes more important to be able to recover just the right piece of compiled knowledge. This requires the use of more sophisticated recovery mechanisms. As this happens the system is likely to rely more on procedural methods than on those of declarative or functional languages. In practice it has been the case with commercial applications that they are first worked out in LISP or prolog and then production versions are written in C. This is a quite natural recognition of the transition frpom an experimental system to a more robust one. Itself an example of a transition from use of compiled knowledge to declarative knowledge.

Expert system shells should thus be considered as special purpose representation-reason-language systems. They usually provide a preferred way of representing knowledge and a preferred language for manipulating the information in the system. As a consequnce there is a preferred way of reasoning about the problem that the system is being used for. Indeed many shells are so constructed that they can only be used for a few types of expert system application precisely because the language and the knowledge representation restrict the reasoning capabilities.

It seems likely that in the future large systems will be built in such a way that the knowledge representation and language will be specifically designed so as to be flexible enough to permit many different reasoning methods to co-exist. This may well entail (as it does in Cyc) allowing two related languages to co-exist in the same system. By using two or more languages one can allow a single representation such as a frame based one to incorporate the knowledge required for more than one reasoning system.

The other major development that can be expected is the development of parallel languages for use in Artificial intelligence applications. Already there are parallel versions of LISP and Prolog. It is interesting that these languages tend to have a semantics that is somewhat different from their single threaded counterparts. These developments can be expected to effect considerable changes in the structure of intelligent systems. The blackboard architecture and neural networks are but the first indications of what can be expected to happen here.

Bibliography

[1] Harold Abelson. Turtle Geometry. MIT Press. 1981

[2] S. Amarel, On the Representations of Problems of Reasoning About Actions. in "Machine Intelligence" Ed D. Michie. American Elsevir. New York 1968

[3] J. Avenhaus and K. Madlener. Term Rewriting and Equational Reasoning. In Formal Techniques in Artificial Intelligence: A Sourcebook. R.B.Banerji Ed. Elsevir. 1990 p1-43.

[4] R.B. Banerji, Artificial Intelligence: A Theoretical Approach., North-Holland, Amsterdam, 1983

[5] R.B. Banerji, Solving the Linguistic Problems in Learning, Fundamenta Informaticae, XII, 51-78, 1989

[6] R.B. Banerji, GPS and the Psychology of the Rubik Cubist: A Study in Reasoning about Actions., In Artificial and Human Intelligence, Eds. R.B. Banerji and Alec Elithorn. North-Holland, Amsterdam, 1983

[7] R.B. Banerji. Learning Theories in a Subset of a Polyadic Logic, Proc. Workshop on Computational Learning Theory, (Haussler and Pitt, Eds.) pp. 267-279, Morgan Kaufmann, 1988.

[8] R.B. Banerji and G.W. Ernst, A Theory for the Complete Mechanization of a GPS Type Problem Solver, In Proc. 5th International Conference on Artificial Intelligence Cambridge MA. 1977

[9] R.B. Banerji. Heuristics, Minimum Distance and a Strange State of the Five-Puzzle, Intelligent Systems: State of the Art and Future Directions (Ras and Zemankova, Eds.), Ellis Horwood, N.Y.(1990).

[10] P. Benjamin, A Method for Creating Heirachical Representations that Serialize Subgoals, Technical Report Philips Laboratories, Briarcliffe NY, 1988

[11] P. Benjamin, L. Dorst, I. Mandhyan and M. Rosar, An Introduction to the Decomposition of Task Representations in Autonomous Systems, In Change of Representation and Inductive Bias, Ed. Paul Benjamin. Kluwer Academic, Boston MA, 1990

[12] L. Bobrow and M. Arbib. Discrete Mathematics. Saunders 1974.

[13] D. Bochvar, On Three-valued Logical Calculus and its Application to the Analysis of Contradictions, Mat. Sbornik, 4, 353-369 1939

[14] R.S. Boyer and J.S. Moore, A Computational Logic Academic Press, New York 1979

[15] Ronald J. Brachman, On the Epistemological Status of Semantic Networks, In Associative Networks: Representation and Uses of Knowledge by Computers, 3 - 50, Ed. N.V. Findler, Academic Press New York, 1979

[16] Ronald J. Brachman and Hector J. Levesque, Readings in Knowledge Representation, Morgan-Kauffman, Los Altos CA. 1985

[17] Ivan Bratko. Prolog Programming for Artificial Intelligence. Second Edition. Addison-Wesley 1990.

[18] Ivan Bratko. Fast Prototyping of Expert Systems using Prolog. In Topics in Expert System Design: Methodologies and Tools. Eds. G. Guida and C. Tasso. North-Holland 1989 pp 69-86.

[19] Timothy Budd, Blending Imperative and Relational Programming. IEEE Software. 8(1). 58-65. 1991.

[20] Rod Burstall and Joseph Goguen. Putting Theories together to Make Specifications. In Raj Reddy, Editor, Proceedings, Fifth International Conference on Artificial Intelligence, 1045 -1048, 1977.

[21] Jaime G. Carbonell. Learning by Analogy: Formulating and Generalizing Plans from Past Experience. In Machine Learning an Artificial Intelligence Apporach Eds. Ryszard S. Michalski, Jaime G. Carbonell and Tom M. Mitchell Tioga Publishing Company. Palo Alto California 1983 pp137-161.

[22] D. Chapman, Planning for Conjunctive Goals, Artificial Intelligence, 32, 333-377 1987

[23] E. Charniak and D. McDermott, Introduction to Artificial Intelligence, Addison-Wesley, Reading MA, 1984

[24] William Clocksin and Chris Mellish, Programming in Prolog, Springer-Verlag, New York, 1984

[25] Jacques Cohen, Constraint Logic programming Languages. Commun ACM 33 (1990) No. 7. pp 52-68.

[26] Paul R. Cohen and Edward A. Feigenbaum, The Handbook of AI. Wiliam Kauffman. Los Altos. CA. 1982.

[27] Alain Colmerauer. An Introduction to Prolog III. Commun. ACM 33 (1990) no. 7. pp 69-90.

[28] Martin Davis, In Defense of First-Order Logic, Talk at First International Symposium on AI and Mathematics, Ft. Lauderdale Florida, January, 1990

[29] Randall Davis, Bruce Buchanan and Edward Shortliffe, Artificial Intelligence, 8, 15 - 45, 1977

[30] B. de Champeau and L. Sint. An Improved bi-directional Search Algorithm. JACM 177-191 1979.

[31] John Debenham, The Implementation of Expert, Knowledge-Based Systems, Proceedings of the Eleventh International Joint conference on Artificial Intelligence, Morgan Kauffman, 1989

[32] John Debenham, Knowledge Systems Design, Prentice Hall, Englewood Cliffs. NJ, 1990

[33] John Debenham, Knowledge Base Design, Australian Computer Journal, 17, 187-196, 1985

[34] L. Dorst, Representations and Algorithms for the $2 \times 2 \times 2$ Rubik's Cube by Half Turns., Technical Report Philips Laboratories, Briarcliffe NY, 1989

[35] G.W. Ernst and M. M. Goldstein, Mechanical Discovery of Classes of Problem Solving Strategies, Journal of the ACM, 29 , 1-23, 1982

[36] H.Ehrig, M. Nagl, G. Rozenberg, and A. Rosenfeld. Eds. Graph Grammars and their applications to Computer Science. Lecture Notes in Computer Science 291. Springer-Verlag NY. 1987

[37] David W. Etherington and Raymond Reiter, On Inheritance Hierarchies with Exceptions, Proceedings AAAI-83 Washington DC, 104-108, 1983

[38] . William Gazdar and Chris Mellish, Natural Language Programming in prolog. Addison-Wesley. Reading MA. 1989.

[39] Michahael R. Genesereth and Nils J. Nilsson, Logical Foundations of Artificial Intelligence, Morgan Kaufmann, Los Altos CA 1987

[40] A. Goldberg and D. Robson. Smalltalk-80: The Language and its Implementation. Addison-Wesley Reading MA. 1983.

[41] Michael J. Gordon, Arthur J. Milner and Christopher P. Wadsworth. Edinburgh LCF. Springer Lecture Notes in Computer Science. 78 1979

[42] Michael J. Gordon, Functional and Imperative Languages: Design and Implementation, Pitman 1988

[43] D. Gries, The Science of Programming, Springer-Verlag, New York, 1983

[44] H.A. Guvenir and G.W. Ernst, Learning Problem Solving Strategies Using Refinement and Macro Generation, Artificial Intelligence.44 209-243 1990.

[45] P.E. Hart and N.J. Nilsson and B. Raphael, A Formal Basis for the Heuristic Determination of Minimum Cost Paths, IEEE Trans. Systems Science and Cyberetics, 100-107, 1968

[46] T.P. Hart and D.J. Edwards, The Tree Prune (TP) Algorithm, Technical Report MIT, Artificial Intelligence Project Memo #30, 1968

[47] Pat Hayes. The Naive Physics Manifesto. In Expert Systems in the Micro-Electronic Age. Ed. D. Michie. Edinburgh University press. Edinburgh. Scotland. 1979

[48] B. Hayes-Roth. The Blackboard Architecture for Control. AI 26 251-321.

[49] J.P.E. Hodgson. Solving Problems by Subproblem Classification. Proceedings ISMIS Torino. 1988.

[50] J.P.E. Hodgson. Interactive Problem Solving. SIGART Newsletter. 1987.

[51] J.P.E. Hodgson, Automatic Generation of Heuristics, In Formal Methods in Artificial Intelligence: A Sourcebook, Ed. R.B. Banerji, Elsevir, New York, 123-171, 1989

[52] J.P.E. Hodgson. Pushouts and Problem Solving. In preliminary proceedings of the First International Workshop on Category Theory in AI. Tarrytown New York May 1989.

[53] J.A.W. Kamp. Instants and Temporal Reference, In: Semantics from Different Points of View, Ed. A. Von Stechow. Springer Verlag 1978.

[54] S. Kleene. Introduction to MetaMathematics. Van Nostrand 1952

[55] R. Korf. Depth First Iterative-Deepening: An Optimal Admissible Tree Search. Artificial Intelligence 27 (1985) 97-109.

[56] R. Korf Planning as Search: A Quantitative Approach. AI 33 1987 65-88

[57] R. Korf. Learning to Solve Problems by Macro-generation. Pitman 1985.

[58] R. Korf. Toward a model of Representation Changes. AI. 14 41-78 1980.

[59] K. Krohn and J. Rhodes. Algebraic Theory of Machines. Trans. AMS 116. 450-464 1965.

[60] J.E.Laird, A. Newell, P.S. Rosenbloom, SOAR: An Architecture for General intelligence. AI 33 1987 1-64.

[61] J.E. Laird, A. Newell, P.S. Rosenbloom. Universal Subgoaling and Chunking. Kluwer Academic publishers. 1986

[62] J. Lambek and P. Scott, Introduction to Higher Order Categorical Logic. Cambridge University Press. 1986.

[63] J-L. Lauriere. A Language and a Program for Stating and Solving Combinatorial Problems. AI 10 1978 29-127

[64] D. Lenat The nature of Heuristics II AI 21 (1-2) 1983 31-59

[65] D. Lenat The nature of heuristics III AI 21 1-2 61-98. 1983

[66] Douglas B. Lenat and R.V. Guha. Building Large Knowledge-Based Systems. Addison-Wesley. Reading MA. 1990.

[67] V. Lesser, Jasmin Pavlin and Edmund Durfee. Approximate Processing in Real Time problem Solving. AI Magazine. 9 1988 49-61.

[68] J. Lukasiewicz. Many-valued Systems of Propositional Logic. In McCall. S. *Polish logic* Oxford 1967.

[69] Anthony S. Maida and Stuart C. Shapiro, Intentsional Concepts in Propositional Semantic Networks, Cognitive Science , 6, 291-330 , 1982

[70] John McCarthy. Programs with Common Sense. In Semantic Information Processing 403-418, Ed. M. Minsky, Cambridge, MA. The MIT Press, 1968. Reprinted in Readings in Knowledge Representation 299-307, Eds. Ronald J. Brachman and Hector J. Levesque. Los Altos, CA. Morgan Kauffman 1985.

[71] Marvin Minsky, A Framework for Representing Knowledge. In P. Winston Ed. The Psychology of Computer Vision. 211-277. McGraw Hill. 1975.

[72] Bernhard Nebel. Reasoning and Revision in Hybrid Representation Systems. Springer Lecture Notes in AI. 422 1990.

[73] Constantin Virgil Negoita. Expert Systems and Fuzzy Systems. Menlo Park CA. Benjamin Cummings 1985.

[74] A. Newell and H.A. Simon. Human Problem Solving. Prentice-Hall. Englewood Cliffs. NJ. 1972.

[75] Penny Nii. The Blackboard Model Of Problem Solving. AI Magazine Vol 7 No 2 p38 - 53 1986

[76] Penny Nii. The Blackboard Model Of Problem Solving. AI Magazine Vol 7 No 3 p82 - 106 1986

[77] S. Niizuma and T. Kitahashi. A Problem Solving Method Using Differences or Equivalence Relations Between States. AI 25 1985 117-151

[78] P. O'Rorke, LT Revisited: Explanation Based Learning and the Logic of Principia Mathematica, Machine Learning, 4, 117 - 159. 1989,

[79] J. Pearl Heuristics Addison-Wesley 1984.

[80] I. Pohl, First Results on the Effect of Error in Heuristic Search, In B. Meltzer and D. Michie (Eds.), Machine Intelligence 5 (American Elsevir) New York 1970. 219-236.

[81] Axel Poigné, Elements of categorical Reasoning: Products and Coproducts and some (co-)limits. In Category Theory and Computer Science. Ed. D.Pitt, S.Abramsky, A. Poigné and D.Rydehead. Springer Lecture Notes in Computer Science. 240 1986.

[82] Axel Poigné, Foundations are Rich Institutions, but Institutions are Poor Foundations, In Categorical Methods in Computer Science, Springer Lecture Notes in Computer Science 393, Springer-Verlag, Heidelberg, 1989

[83] J.R. Quinlan and E.B. Hunt. A Formal Deductive Problem-Solving System. Journal of the ACM. 15 (1968) 625-646.

[84] R. Reiter, A Logic for Default Reasoning, Artificial Intelligence, 13(1-2) , 81-132 , 1980

[85] Stuart J. Russell. The Use of Knowledge in Analogy and Induction. Pitman. London 1989.

[86] Sacerdoti. Earl D. The Non-linear Nature of Plans. Advance papers 4th International Joint Conference on Artificial Intelligence. Tbilisi 1975 Vol 1 206-214.

[87] Selfridge Oliver G. Pandemonium: A Paradigm for Learning. Proceedings of the Symposium on the Mechanization of Thought Processes. 511-529. Eds. D.V.Blake and A.M. Uttley. London H.M. Stationary Office. 1959.

[88] Roger C. Schank and Robert P. Abelson, Scripts, Plans, Goals and Underanding, Lawrence Erlbaum Associates, New York, 1977

[89] S.C. Shapiro, A net structure for semantic information storage deduction, and retrieval, In Proceedings of the 2nd International Joint Conference on Artificial Intelligence, 512-523 , 1971

[90] Lokendra Shastri, Semantic Networks: An Evidential Formalization and Its Connectionist Realization, Pitman, London, England, 1987

[91] J.F. Sowa, Conceptual Structures: Information processing in Mind and Machine, Addison-Wesley, Reading, MA, 1984

[92] Leon Sterling and Ehud Shapiro, The Art of prolog, MIT Press, Cambridge MA, 1986

[93] Guy Steele, Common LISP Reference Manual, Digital Press, Bradford, MA, 1984

[94] B. Stroustrup. The C++ programming Language. Addsion-Wesley Reading MA. 1986.

[95] Gerald J. Sussman. A Computer Model of Skill Acquisition. American Elsevier. New York 1975.

[96] M. Tambe, A. Newell and P.S. Rosenbloom. The Problem of Expensive Chunks and its Solution by Restricting Expressiveness. Machine Learning. 5 299-348 1990

[97] Raymond Turner. Logics for Artificial Intelligence. Chichester. Ellis Horwood 1984.

[98] D.H.D. Warren, Implementing Prolog - Compiling Logic Programs 1 and 2, DAI Research Reports 39 and 40. University of Edinburgh, 1977.

[99] Richard W. Weyrauch, Prolegomena to a Theory of Mechanized Formal Reasoning AI 13 1980 133-170 Reprinted in Readings in Knowledge Representation 299-307, Eds. Ronald J. Brachman and Hector J. Levesque. Los Altos, CA. Morgan Kauffman 1985.

[100] R. Wilensky, Lispcraft, Norton, New York, 1983

[101] Patrick H. Winston and Berthold Laus Henry Horn, LISP, Addison-Wesley, Cambridge, MA, 1984

[102] William A. Woods, What's in a Link: Foundations for Semantic Networks, In Representation and Understanding: Studies in Cognitive Science, Eds. D.G. Bobrow and A.M. Collins, New York. Academic Press 1975.

[103] Lofti A. Zadeh. Fuzzy Sets. Information and Control 8 338- 353 1965

[104] Lofti A. Zadeh. Fuzzy Logic and Approximate reasoning. Synthese 30 407-428 1975.

Index

DATE DUE

DEC 0 9 1994	